LAST LONG RIDE

A JOURNEY OF FREEDOM, ADVENTURE, AND
LOVE ENDS WHERE IT ALL BEGAN

FILIPE MASETTI LEITE

Project Manager: Peter Hawkins

Editorial assistance by Gari Strawn of strawnediting.com.

Cover art by Noexcuse Marketing Estratégico

Cover photo by Clara Victoria Davel.

Ebook ISBN 978-1-927607-87-9

Paperback ISBN 978-1-927607-86-2

LAST LONG RIDE

A Journey of Adventure, Freedom, and Love
Ends Where It All Began

Filipe Masetti Leite

To Clara Victoria Davel, my flor del pago. I love you, amor.

Mac and Smokey, my wild horses.

FOREWORD BY CUCHULLAINE O'REILLY

AUTHOR OF THE ENCYCLOPEDIA OF EQUESTRIAN TRAVEL

Set aside your expectations. If you are searching for an armchair adventure, you'll get your money's worth because within these pages is far more than your average action-packed pony picnic. More importantly, this is a timeless tale about a unique friendship that crosses centuries, traverses nations, and unites humanity via that single magic word: *horse*.

In September 1924, an inexperienced young man named Aimé Tschiffely swung into the saddle and set off to ride 10,000 miles from Buenos Aires, Argentina to New York, NY. The Argentine press mocked him as a suicidal Don Quixote with two old horses and not a chance in hell. The skeptics changed their minds as the world witnessed the unfolding of a Cinderella story that has passed into modern legend.

Tschiffely faced every type of danger the Americas could throw at him. The deadly "Horse Killer Desert" of Chile, Peru's towering Andes Mountains, and the snake-infested jungles of Columbia lay ahead. So did suffocating heat, bloody revolutions, tropical diseases, vampire bats, poisonous plants, and hostile border guards. Nothing and no one stopped Tschiffely!

By the time he reached the United States after three years in the saddle, Tschiffely's reputation had been transformed from lunatic to extraordinary equestrian explorer. He was invited to meet President Coolidge at the White House. He spoke to an entranced audience at the National Geographic Society and rode on to New York City where he was honored by a ticker tape parade.

Then, like the modest hero that he was, Tschiffely shipped his loyal horses home to Argentina and wrote *Tschiffely's Ride,* the twentieth century's most influential equestrian travel book. That tale inspired four generations to follow Aimé's example, but it took a hundred years before an extraordinary youth undertook a Homeric journey in search of his Long Rider hero. Swiss Long Rider Aimé Tschiffely inspired Brazilian Long Rider Filipe Leite.

As the founder of the Long Riders' Guild, I have mentored more than 200 equestrian explorers who have crossed every continent except Antarctica. For decades, thousands of messages seeking advice have arrived at the Guild, yet I clearly recall that Thursday, July 21, 2011, when a young man wrote to say that he was determined, as Aimé had said, "to taste the salt of life," no matter what it cost.

"As a young child, I fell absolutely in love with Tschiffely's story and dreamed of making my own equestrian journey. This idea has never left my mind, so in June of 2012, I will set off to ride 16,000 kilometers from Canada to my family's home in Brazil," Filipe Leite wrote.

At the Long Riders' Guild, we deal with the reality, not the romance, of equestrian travel. We ask hard questions and enforce a strict code of ethics. Filipe was required to clarify his equestrian experience, outline his travel plans, show his proposed route, and verify details about his horses and equipment. Only when Filipe had demonstrated his willingness to put the horse's safety before his ego and to promote the Guild's philosophy of Harmonious Horsemanship was he granted our trust.

To reduce his costs, the Guild provided one of its adjustable pack saddles so as to diminish the risk of injury to the packhorse. More importantly, we asked Filipe to carry the Guild flag across the Americas, an honor reserved only for the most dangerous and important journeys. Even I could not have foreseen that this flag would spend eleven years traveling 25,000 kilometers from Yukon Territory, Alaska, to distant Tierra del Fuego, Patagonia.

What happened became a three-part passage across North, Central, and South America. Filipe's first book, *Long Ride Home*, recounted enough adventures to rival Tschiffely. For example, after departing in 2012, there was the incident when he was required to ride through a region of Mexico so lawless that he was surrounded and escorted by a squad of heavily armed federal troops. Brazil gave her native son a hero's welcome when he rode into the family town of Espírito Santo do Pinhal in 2014.

With more than 9,000 miles behind him, most people expected Filipe to hang up his saddle. They didn't understand how deeply the journey had transformed his soul. That's why I wasn't surprised when Filipe set off in 2016 to ride nearly 5,000 miles to Ushuaia, the very tip of the South American continent. His second book, *Long Ride to the End of the World,* revealed how, in the scorched Patagonian landscape, Filipe unexpectedly found the love of his life.

To me, it was obvious what would happen next. To complete the Tschiffely Trilogy, Filipe would need to ride from Alaska south into Canada where it all began. He set off on his third journey in 2019 and arrived in Calgary, Canada, in 2020. With 25,000 kilometers under his saddle, even his hero Aimé Tschiffely had not ridden so far.

Aimé had ridden north, and Filipe had traveled south. Aimé inspired a wave of twentieth-century imitators. Yet, in an ironic twist of fate, Filipe encountered a host of antagonistic governments that effectively blocked the ancient trail across the Americas. Without knowing it, Filipe had become the last Long Rider to follow Tschiffely's Trail.

On February 3, 2022, I received another email from Filipe. Only this wasn't a message from an apprehensive youth. This was a request from a serious man who had stared down death, crossed continents, and suffered in the saddle, just like his hero Aimé Tschiffely.

"CuChullaine, only you understand what I have accomplished and endured during the past decade. Only you have the knowledge of

Tschiffely and Long Rider history to place my journey into perspective. Would you write the foreword to my third book?"

I agreed to do so because of one essential reason. In response to a request that I made to him in 2012, Filipe had documented the effects of climate change across the Americas. His journey had barely begun across the USA when he had trouble finding water and grazing for his horses. In Central America, he observed waves of desperate climate refugees trudging north in search of food and salvation. In Patagonia, he saw how once rich grassland was becoming desert. And finally, in formerly cold Yukon, Filipe documented how an ancient glacier had receded, and a famous river had disappeared.

He wrote in this book, *The Last Long Ride:* "With my head tilted down, I felt that sand hit me in the face for the hour it took me to cross the valley on horseback. It was apocalyptic. The lake, which had receded a full kilometer to leave islands standing completely out of the water, was otherworldly and sad."

During his years in the saddle, Filipe lectured to children in Canada, the United States, Mexico, Guatemala, Honduras, Nicaragua, Costa Rica, Peru, Bolivia, Brazil, Uruguay, and Argentina. He told them about how the climate was changing, but he balanced that fact with the encouraging message that any of them could swing into the saddle and follow their own dream, no matter how distant it might seem.

Aimé Tschiffely died the month I was born in 1954. I protect his legend. I know his story well. That is why I feel confident that if Aimé were alive he would be proud of Filipe. I know I am.

CuChullaine O'Reilly, FRGS
    Founder, The Long Riders' Guild
    Executor, The Tschiffely Literary Estate

1

THE JOURNEY BEFORE THE JOURNEY

Espirito Santo do Pinhal, Brazil

On April 1, 2019, Clara and I were two fools trying to fit clothing and equipment into four worn-out suitcases for a yearlong Long Ride.

"I hate packing," I complained every three minutes. She laughed at me as I sorted a saddle, saddle pads, reins, cameras, a drone, batteries, gloves, pants, shirts, and socks. It took a couple of hours to shove everything into our four large bags that had to weigh thirty-two kilograms or less. It was painful. After an entire year of planning, we were one day away from flying to Canada to begin training the horses I would ride on this final journey from Alaska to Calgary.

"I can't believe we leave tomorrow." My beautiful Argentinian girl-friend stared at our planning wall. It was covered in white poster board, scrawled with long lists of equipment, paperwork, dates, and sponsors. *CANADA - BRAZIL* was written across the top in colorful letters.

"*Mañana*." I smiled before giving her a long hug. Tomorrow.

I met Clara in El Bolsón, Patagonia, during my second Long Ride to Ushuaia. I fell in love with her at first sight. She had the upturned eyes of a cat, her irises were bright honey, with a darker spot on the bottom of her left iris. She had thick dark eyebrows, sexy lips, and dark skin that made her look like a Spanish princess from a bygone era. Her jet-black hair, her perfect body, and her bemused gaze enchanted me. She was a lioness, strong and intense. She wore a black tank top and ripped, paint-splattered jean shorts. She was Salma Hayek in her heyday!

There wasn't a lick of makeup on her face. No blush. No eyeliner. No lipstick. Her nails weren't painted. She didn't bother to put on any perfume. All this and yet she was the most beautiful woman I ever laid eyes on. At that moment, I realized why I fell in love with this girl so quickly. She was so pure, so genuine, naturally gorgeous like a Patagonian sunrise. It was as if I could see through her skin and into her soul, an old soul whose name was Truth.

But there was so much more that drew me to her. Clara is smart, charming, and emits a light that shines bright. She is one of those women who was born to be a mother: responsible, caring, kind-hearted, tender, and thoughtful. She is the kind of person every child and animal in the room wants to get close to. It is as if she has a magnet that pulls the pure of heart to her. The bold Argentinian is also very resourceful. She understands engines and cars, can plant and grow anything with roots, and will knit an intricate sweater before you can tack a horse.

It wasn't easy winning this *gaucha* over, but since cowboys don't have any quit in them, eventually I managed to lasso the love of my life. After dating long-distance for two years, this new journey would be our first major test.

Before we made our way to the dining room to join my family waiting with a delicious *feijoada* (bean and meat stew) and cold beers, I made a prediction, "Either we kill one another in the far north or we fall even more in love."

Seated around the dinner table, we shared stories, talked about this new adventure, and laughed the night away. It was amazing having them there for one final hurrah. I tried to take in their energy, savoring it. It would be many long months before I saw them again. That was if I didn't get eaten by a bear or freeze to death.

After we shared a tight hug, my ninety-two-year-old grandmother told me, "Go with God, my son. I will light a candle for you and your new horses, and you will see, everything will work out."

With her perfectly styled, voluminous pixie-cut brown hair, perfume smelling of baby powder, pearl necklace, and matching earrings, she placed both of her cold and brittle hands on my face before we separated. Her moist eyes, small and droopy, seemed to carry the wisdom of the world. "*Filho* (son)," she said one final time in her strong raspy voice.

"*Amém, avó,*" I responded. Amen. I hoped her small white candle and her enormous faith in God would keep us safe in the north.

My mother wasn't as optimistic. "Filipe, what do you mean you can't carry a gun? There are so many bears up there and they eat people!"

I couldn't blame her. This would be the third time I'd made the selfless and caring brunette worry sick for more than 365 days as I rode horses through wild and trackless regions of the world. Trying to sound like I believed the words I spoke, I said, "I'll be fine, Mom."

"I'm going to ride into Calgary with you," my dad said. It was nice!

The following morning, we began the journey that always took place before the actual journey. The first stage was a two and a half hour drive to the Guarulhos Airport in São Paulo. We were accompanied by my sisters Paolla and Izeballa and my mother Claudia. We arrived on time, and luckily, all our bags were under the weight limit.

"Don't cry, Iza, we'll see each other soon," I said to my little sister as she shed heavy tears. I must admit, I love my entire family to death, but being apart from Iza was by far the hardest thing. Children grow and change so quickly. When I am away from her for one or two years and I see her again, she is almost a different person. Taller, more confident, more of an adult and less a child. The first time I saw her when I arrived in Brazil after my first Long Ride from Canada, she touched my face with her gentle little fingers as if trying to remember who I was. It had been more than three years since I had last seen her. She had gone from a squirmy five-year-old little girl to a tall nine-year-old kid. It really hits home that I will never be able to get the time back that I spent away from my loved ones. Every project comes with sacrifices.

Before Clara and I entered the Boeing 787-9, a dear friend, Naira at Air Canada, who had been following all my journeys, announced that Clara and I would be upgraded and flying to Toronto first-class.

"What, what? I can't believe it!" Clara said with a wide smile on her tanned face. Sitting in seat 1-A, I enjoyed a glass of prosecco while reading the dinner menu and all of its courses. Clara sat in 1-B and pressed all the buttons on her comfy seat and took photos to send to her family back in Argentina. It may have made the news all the way back in El Bolsón!

After the ten-hour flight, and yes, I slept like a rock in my seat that turned into a bed, we arrived in the Great White North.

"Welcome to Canada," my friends Peter Hawkins and Arnon Melo said as they met us outside Pearson airport. Longtime friends who had become family, they were my first sponsors for my first ride from Canada to Brazil and even flew down to Barretos when I arrived. We drove to their gorgeous home in Etobicoke where we spent three nights.

"We are thinking of meeting you guys in Alaska for a few days," Peter announced over dinner that night. His news made Clara and me glow with joy.

The next morning, I was excited to show Clara Toronto, but more importantly, I wanted her to meet my best friends. From the moment we met in Patagonia, two years earlier, I raved about them. I moved to Canada with my family at the age of nine. This great nation and its people were very important to understanding who I became. Although I do not hold a Canadian passport, yet, in many ways, this was my home.

We climbed the CN Tower, visited Ripley's Aquarium, and walked the streets of Kensington Market together. It felt so nice to show her around the city where I spent my formative years and that I love so much. I also had the opportunity to show her Bolton, the small town where I grew up.

"That's where I went to elementary school," I told her as we drove by Holy Family. But, by far, the best part was introducing her to my best friends, the guys I grew up with. On a clear Friday night, we met at my friend Eric Forsyth's studio, went out for dinner, and then hit the town. It was perfect. My best friends by my side...the love of my life with me...a beautiful Toronto spring night.

"If you don't marry her, I will, bro!" my best friend Mark Maw announced with his arm over my shoulder. I was euphoric to spend time with Eric Robertson (Pappi), Kyle Kellett (Kelly), Mathew Mazzaferro (Fuego), Ryan Spillar (Spills), Derrick Nield (Clutch), John Sousa (J-sous), Terry Indellicato (Two Shots), Ian Dixon (Dicky), Michael Heslin (Healing), Trevor Franklin, David Greco, and their loved ones. I wish that night could have lasted forever.

Unfortunately, it couldn't. The following morning at 9 a.m., we were on a flight to Calgary. I was hungover. Clarita was not. She doesn't drink.

"Welcome to Calgary," Zane Aitken said. The blond built like a football player offered me a firm handshake. Zane, the son of Marie and Rocky, picked us up from the airport and drove us two hours south to his parent's ranch in Claresholm. The couple, who had been following my ride since I left Calgary in 2012, offered to lend us their motorhome as a support vehicle for this final ride. Memories flooded back as we drove down Highway 2, the same road I took when I left Calgary on horseback headed for Brazil seven years earlier. These were the first kilometers I traveled on my first journey. To be back to this area en route to my third Long Ride felt simply unbelievable, as if I were in the middle of a dream.

Before we pulled into the driveway, I spotted our new home. The 1990 Ford Econoline was bought by Marie and her husband Rocky just for our journey. The old, off-yellow motorhome stuck out like a sore thumb in the front yard of their ranch. To many, it may have looked like an ugly square structure from the past. To me, it was the most beautiful and comforting sight. Only I knew the pain and suffering it would keep me from feeling.

After we hugged, I told Marie, "I will never be able to thank you properly."

Marie was pale, had gray hair down to her shoulders, usually tied in two braids, and wore reading glasses. She spoke softly most of the time, but could be assertive when she wanted to get her point across.

Adjusting her glasses, the horsewoman and nurse told me, "I know you would do the same for my children, and I just love what you are doing."

The truth is, I really won't be able to ever thank this family properly. Who does this? Who goes out of their way, spends their money, just to help another human being with a project — a dream? Marie and Rocky were about to change our lives.

At twenty-five, when I rode out of the Centennial Calgary Stampede Rodeo on that scorching July morning in 2012, I had never gone on a Long Ride before. I had no idea where I would sleep that night, never mind how I would actually manage to make it to Brazil alive. I had 16,000 kilometers of doubts and fears ahead of me. The anxiety nearly drove me mad. All my equipment had to fit in my pack saddle and, since my horses carried it, had to weigh less than 150 pounds. I traveled for 803 days and only had a support vehicle in the southern United States to carry water for the horses.

I made it to my hometown in Brazil with the bare minimum. From my toothbrush to my underwear, to camera equipment, to horse medication, everything had to have a real value or it stayed behind. If we couldn't find water, my horses and I didn't drink. It was both dangerous and painful, especially the solitude I endured at certain points. For instance, in Wyoming I crossed a dry and desolate mountain without seeing another human being for five days. Unable to find water, I had to give my horses cooking oil at night and pray that they didn't colic.

In Argentina, my second Long Ride, I rode hundreds of kilometers through scorched lands. Officials estimated more than 80,000 head of cattle were killed and over 2 million hectares of land burned. Horses, dogs, and houses were lost in fires lit by electrical storms.

One *gaucho* told me during that stretch, "I tried to release my horses in time, but when I got to my farm, it was too late." A single tear tracked down his dusty face.

For 170 kilometers, smoke blocked the sky. The sun only seeped through, a deep orange above us. The ponies and I fought to breathe as high winds blew smoke and ash into our faces all day. My eyes stung and the back of my throat burned. On both sides of the highway, what was once tall green, yellow, and brown grass was now black tar and gray ash.

The night before arriving in Rio Colorado, I had only one 500 milliliter bottle of water left. I found an unlocked corral where I set up my tent and sipped my water slowly. With parched lips and a dry throat, I wanted to chug the bottle, but I knew I would need it the next day.

Feeling completely vulnerable and dirtier than a chimney sweep, I watched an old truck drive up and park in front of the gate. A tall, grimacing man jumped out. "Who allowed you to enter?" he demanded as I approached him.

"No one, sir," I answered. "I saw the gate wasn't locked and let myself in." As I explained my journey to him, he looked me up and down in silence.

"Okay, I guess you can spend the night, but if the owner comes, you tell him you spoke to me."

Relieved, the tension in my shoulders eased. I asked if I could drink the water from the nearby windmill. He said no because of sulfate levels. We shook hands and he walked towards his truck as I headed to my tent, my head hanging low. Staring at the rocky soil, I heard a yell. When I looked up, the man, who minutes earlier I expected to swallow me alive, was holding a liter bottle of frozen water in his hand. I ran up, grabbed the bottle, and thanked him.

Later, alone in my tent watching the horses graze, I cried silently, holding that cold bottle against my left cheek. The icy plastic gave my burned skin momentary relief. It was just water. It seems ridiculous for someone to cry over a liter of frozen water, but I had been so desperate moments earlier.

Thankfully, that suffering was behind me. With this expedition, thanks to Marie and Rocky, things would be different. In the motorhome, driven by Clara, we could carry lightweight panels to build a corral for the horses every night, water, feed, and hay. I would be able to sleep in a real bed. Most importantly, I'd have someone to share this journey with.

Marie gave us the tour of our new home, and Rocky went about explaining the mechanics. The retired Health Safety and Environmental Manager was quirky and, like most of the fathers I had met, hardworking. He loved his dogs and always had a wrench in his hand. "You have to wear gloves. This will save your life," he would tell us as he fixed something in the shop.

After a delicious steak dinner that evening, we began loading our clothing and equipment into the Econoline.

"Socks will go here, shirts will hang in that closet, food will go in this cabinet..." Clara and I were so happy to be organizing our little home-on-wheels for the next year.

We had been dating long-distance since meeting at her home in El Bolsón, Argentina, in 2017. It was hard, but we tried to see each other as much as possible. Every couple of months, I would fly down to Patagonia or she would travel to Brazil. Now, for the first time in two years of dating, we would be together 24/7. It felt exquisite and a little scary.

Clara was in her first year of Environmental Management at Blas Pascal University in Bariloche. Luckily, she was studying online, so while she helped me during this Last Long Ride, she could continue her studies from the far north. Happy with anticipation as she organized her school material, she exclaimed, "Look! My books fit perfectly into this cabinet."

The following morning, we drove to Lethbridge to get the motorhome insured and certified. It should have been a straightforward process. Unfortunately, it turned into a nightmare.

"Your motorhome has been written off, sir," a sour-faced man in his mid-forties told Rocky. "You need to take it through a salvage inspection by a licensed technician before we can certify it."

It was a silent dinner back in Claresholm. Less than twenty-four hours after putting our socks into the drawers of our motorhome, we were taking them out and packing our bags again.

"Well, it was nice while it lasted," I said, trying to lighten the mood. It didn't work. We no longer had a home.

"I talked to Marie, and you guys need to get to those horses ASAP," Rocky told us. "Take our old truck, and we will see what happens with the motorhome. If it passes the inspection next week, we will drive it out. If it doesn't, you can borrow our truck and use it as a support vehicle."

Rocky was right. I needed to start working with the horses right away. We packed our things into the back of their white Ford F-150, covered it with a blue tarp, and drove over the Rocky Mountains to southern British Columbia. The drive ended up being one of the most beautiful I have ever taken in my life. Clara and I took two days to drive the 731 kilometers because we stopped so much to film and take photos. The stunning scenery helped take the edge off.

"Welcome to Penticton, you guys," Sara Turner greeted us before we shared a hug.

She began to cry immediately. "I'm so sad, Filipe," she said, heavy tears running down her face. Sara's mare, Deedee, had passed away a few days earlier. She knew I understood her loss. Deedee was one of the horses she used to ride with me for a month into Nicaragua during my first Long Ride.

I gave her a bottle of Crown Royal at once, and we picked up where we last left off years ago in Central America.

2

THE WILD HORSES ARE VERY WILD

W hen I met Sara in Tegucigalpa, Honduras, during my ride from Canada to Brazil, she talked my ear off about how amazing her wild horse Honey was. "I grew up riding this mare everywhere. She is the best horse in the world," Sara told me as we rode south together.

Sara was a thin, blonde firecracker who would rather lose a friend before missing a joke. She also had the biggest heart in the world and helped everyone around her. In 2013, she not only rode with me into Nicaragua, she also helped me care for my horse, Bruiser, when he was hurt. Sara allowed the tall sorrel gelding to rest at her ranch in Honduras where she taught underprivileged children how to ride and jump. She became a friend for life thanks to our shared love for the horse and our adventure together.

The Canadian cowgirl loved her wild horse Honey so much she actually flew her down to Honduras from Canada. I had the pleasure of meeting Honey and was impressed by her big bones and strong hooves. When the time came to find the horses for my Last Long Ride, Sara, who had moved back to Penticton, British Columbia, convinced me to take two horses with the same origins as Honey. "These are the animals you need for this wild terrain, Filipe. They will keep you alive," Sara assured me as we spoke about the opportunity over Skype.

I agreed. The instincts these wild horses had acquired over generations of survival of the fittest would keep us safe against grizzly bears, mountain lions, harsh weather, never-ending muskeg, and mighty mountains.

"Most riders want to buy Quarter Horses, Paints, or Morgans," Sara explained. She also mentioned that a considerable number of wild horses are going to slaughter these days. The only person who bought those horses at auction in recent years was the meat man. Wild horses have lived in western Canada for hundreds of years. They helped build this great nation and contributed to WWII. They were ridden, served as pack animals, and were also food. However, they don't have a "right of place" in the land they inhabit. Many people call for the removal of these "pests."

As we soaked in her mom's hot tub overlooking Okanagan Lake, Sara told me, "You will inspire more people to ride these horses. This is so important."

Drinking way too much Crown Royal, I promised her to do everything in my power to get more wild horses into good homes and out of the slaughterhouse.

Sara purchased a horse for my ride from the Penticton Indian Band. The seller was a great horseman named Two Buck. This was the same herd Honey came from when Sara was still a teen. The tall palomino she named Jughead, for his big head and roman nose, went to a young trainer near Vancouver named Cole. After little more than a month working with the horse, Cole realized we did not have enough time to get him ready for the ride. Jughead, like some mustangs who are removed from their natural habitat, sank into a depression and didn't want to eat or do any work. He simply spent his time sulking.

"Cole said this is normal with some horses, and Jughead needed more time to adapt to his new life," Sara told me over Skype. Only a month before leaving, we had to draw up a new plan. Sara contacted a horse trainer and rancher out of Osoyoos, British

Columbia, forty minutes south of Penticton. He agreed to help us out.

I was still in Brazil when Sara told me, "Aaron Stelkia is going to lend us two of his wildies. We will try to get Jughead out to you when he is ready." She went on to send me photos of a wide-eyed gray by the name of Smokey and a buckskin tank called Coyote. Sara assured me they were broke to ride and castrated. She drove to Osoyoos to meet Aaron and the horses. I trusted her. I should have known better!

The morning after being reunited with Sara, I awoke hungover from too much Crown Royal and beer. "Why am I always waking up hungover when I see you?" I asked Sara as we drove south to Osoyoos. We both laughed.

On a chilly Sunday morning, we made our way to Indian Grove Riding Stables where Aaron Stelkia ran his trail riding business. I was so excited to finally meet my new horses I could hardly wait.

As I daydreamed about riding Coyote and Smokey in this exotic landscape, Sara told me, "You're going to love them."

Suddenly, my daydreaming came to an abrupt end. A police officer signaled for us to pull over. The speed limit was eighty. The speedometer was dropping as Clara, who was driving, hit the brake, it read 123 kilometers per hour. "I told you to drive slow."

Sara sat in the middle seat of the truck Marie and Rocky lent us. She wasn't wearing a seatbelt, but not by choice. There was no seatbelt.

"We are screwed," I said.

"Don't worry, it will be okay," Clara said nervously.

"This isn't Argentina, Clara. This is Canada. Believe me when I say we are screwed." Pondering the cost of the ticket we were about to get, I was fuming.

When the truck came to a complete stop, a grinning officer stepped up to the window. "Hello! You guys in a hurry? Can I see your license and the vehicle's registration, please?"

Clara handed them over. He studied her laminated driver's license from Patagonia, her name and info written with a typewriter. It looked like a library card.

"Sorry, it's from Argentina," she said.

"Okay, I'll be back," he said before walking to his vehicle.

We sat there in agony while we awaited his return. I was so angry I didn't say anything. Sara, who gets nervous at awkward moments, couldn't stop giggling. Clara had a look of fear on her face while she prayed to her gods.

"Okay, I'm only going to give you a warning this time, but please slow down," the officer said before passing her a piece of paper and her documents.

"Thank you," Clara said with a giant smile before turning to me and saying, "I told you so!"

I couldn't believe our good fortune. "What, what the hell just happened?"

"Clara? Did you show him a tit while we weren't looking?" Sara teased, letting out a snort. She laughed so hard. We all joined her. I guess I wasn't the only guy who had eyes for Clarita.

When we arrived at the riding stables, there wasn't time to see anything. Aaron Stelkia and his workers were getting ready to move cattle to another pasture, and they enlisted us to help. I was told my horse for the day was a big sorrel standing in the corner. When I went to grab him, I realized it was going to be an interesting day. He was a tight ball of nerves.

"Don't let him get by you, cut him off," I heard one of the workers yelling behind me as the big-boned animal ran by like a freight train. I eventually caught him, and he danced around me, trying to get away. Tacking him made me realize just how green the animal was. It was touch and go with the brush, the saddle pads, the saddle. He didn't want anything to do with me.

"Have you guys ridden this horse much?" I asked Caley, the manager of the trail riding business.

"Yes, he has had a couple of rides," snapped the skinny redhead, drinking one of her case-a-day Pepsis, not giving me much thought.

After I tacked him, I made him lunge some circles around me and then prayed. I put my left foot into the stirrup. Bending his head to the left with my reins, I jumped on. He did a few circles nervously before I stopped him. I took in a deep breath and let it out slowly before I coaxed him forward gently. Thankfully, he didn't buck, but he was a fearful beast.

All day, I stood on the tips of my toes in the stirrups waiting for the sorrel to explode. He would be fine, pushing cattle for several minutes. Then, all of a sudden, with no heads-up, something would make him take off at a gallop. I held on for dear life until I managed to stop him. It was a fun day, to say the least. We pushed cattle in the only desert in Canada, the northern tip of the Sonora Desert. The surrounding mountains made for a spectacular landscape.

"This is my home. It's beautiful," Aaron Stelkia said from atop his dark bay. "Some people call it a wasteland, but when you come out here on the back of a horse, you see its beauty."

Aaron was a short man with a pale complexion and bright blue eyes. He worked hard, slept little, loved playing poker, and was always sipping on an extra-large cup of coffee. In his strong gaze, his indigenous roots were evident. His mother was Native, and his father came to Canada from Eastern Europe. It was such an amazing opportunity to get to know Aaron and his family for a few days, to learn from him. He was a tremendous horseman who trained his first horse at the age of seven.

He didn't speak much, and when he talked, he usually looked the other way as opposed to looking into my eyes. "My mother was a great horsewoman, and she taught me from an early age," Aaron said, looking out towards the horizon.

After the work was done, we all met at a local diner for dinner. I got to know Caley and her boyfriend Jordan who worked for Aaron and Aaron's mother, Jane. When dinner was over, we drove back to the stables. Aaron kindly allowed Clara and me to sleep in an empty bedroom next to Caley and Jordan, underneath his loft.

"My house burned down last year, so now I'm living here," he told me before we called it a night.

The space had a bathroom, a tack room with over thirty saddles, a large black leather couch, a flatscreen television, a fridge, and two bedrooms. After putting our things away in the room, I was so excited, I went to see my new horses. It was already dark, but I needed to say hello. I very quickly realized Coyote was extremely wild. He didn't let me get anywhere near him and showed clear signs that if I tried, he would kill me. He was so tall, wide, and intimidating, I felt like I was near a bull not a horse.

I grabbed Smokey instead. It took me about fifteen minutes to catch him. When I went to tack the small gray, he was worse than my sorrel gelding from a few hours earlier. Much worse. Eventually, I managed to tighten the cinch while he danced uncomfortably. I tried to put the bit in his mouth. It was as if he had never seen one before. That's when I began to worry.

When I checked under Smokey's back legs using the flashlight on my iPhone, I saw he was not gelded yet. He was still a stud. Then I really began to worry. I tied him back up and went to look at Coyote. It was like approaching a grizzly. I ducked and looked under his back legs from a safe distance. He was also a stud.

After I untacked Smokey, I confessed to Clara, "These horses are two wild and unbroken studs! I'm screwed!"

That night lying in bed, I stared at the white ceiling for hours trying to figure out what to do. We no longer had a motorhome as a support vehicle. My horses were nowhere near ready to go on a Long Ride. They were nowhere near ready to be ridden on the ranch, never mind crossing Alaska and the Yukon. To make matters worse, I had never trained a wild horse before, and we only had two weeks before I had to drive up to Alaska.

"How the hell are we going to do this?" I whispered to the Universe before I dozed off to a fitful sleep.

3

COWBOY UP

My second day at Indian Grove Riding Stables, I did the only thing possible. I had to cowboy up.

I awoke at the crack of dawn and began working with Smokey and Coyote. I had no experience training wild horses, but if I was to begin this journey I would have to learn, and it would have to be done quickly. Aaron helped me as much as he could with direction, but he was working hard with his fencing business and wasn't in the best riding shape. After his son Shaun passed away a few years previously, he had stopped working with these horses altogether.

With sad eyes, he confided, "When my son drowned, I was very depressed. I completely stepped away from training."

Aaron's son rode and trained these animals like his old man. "My boy died two days after he rode this horse for the first time," Aaron said, holding Coyote's lead rope.

The buckskin was literally built like a bull — muscular and stocky. He had a dark mane with patches of light-blond, and his wide body showed signs of the Nordic fjord in his bloodlines. He was stunning to look at, but when you approached him, he would begin to nod his head up and down. It was a warning not to get any closer. If I dared to approach, adrenaline would make my heart race more and more with each step closer. I have never been so scared of a horse in my entire life. He made me question everything I had ever done. He made me feel like a journalist, not a cowboy.

After Shaun passed away, Aaron had released the horse back into the wild where he remained for several years until he returned one day. The horseman caught the horse, and now wanted me to take Coyote on this journey to celebrate his son's life. I loved the story and felt honored to celebrate Shaun's life. It sounded like he was a great kid, but it seemed literally impossible to get the nine-year-old stud ready in only two weeks.

The first day of training, we went into the round pen to work with Coyote. Aaron lunged the wild horse, and he circled the experienced horseman peacefully for a moment. Suddenly, Coyote exploded and ripped the lead rope out of the trainer's hand. The wild horse took off bucking hard, snorting like a devil. After a few spins, he faced Aaron and charged at him as if he was going to attack the trainer.

Clara and I, filming from outside the railing, stopped breathing. Luckily, Aaron kept his cool and stood his ground. He raised his arms and stopped the wild horse in his tracks. He eventually calmed the horse down and continued working with him.

After the chaos waned, Clara observed, "Wow, that was scary!"

That night, I sent Karen Hardy the video of Coyote bucking. She was my American mom who adopted me during my ride from Calgary to Brazil. The next morning, she was at the stables in Osoyoos.

"I can't believe you drove up here from Washington state," I said to Karen after we hugged.

"I flew to Barretos, Brazil to see you cross the finish line. You don't think I would come a few hours north to insure one of my kids didn't get killed?"

Karen, an experienced horsewoman, had trained several mustangs in her lifetime. She even trained Dude, the mustang from the Taos Pueblo Reserve I'd ridden from Texas to Brazil. Dude was one of the kindest horses I ever got the chance to ride. Karen spent the entire day with me working with Smokey and Coyote.

Using varied techniques and tools, we lunged them, put saddles on their backs, and worked on stepping on and off. It was comforting having Karen there to help me. Her motherly love, along with her extensive horse knowledge, made me feel a lot better. "You think I would let one of my kids get hurt? Never!" the powerful cowgirl said before she drove back south.

I continued to work with the two horses with Aaron's guidance and things started to look better, with Smokey anyway. We castrated the little gray horse, and I even managed to get on his back and ride him inside the round pen. Every few seconds, he would take off running like a bat out of hell, but he didn't buck and I stayed on. Unfortunately, on the third day, my coach decided it would be a good idea for him to ride the gray.

With his tall cup of coffee in hand, Aaron announced, "I'm going to get on him this morning." It didn't take long for Smokey to dump the trainer, not once, but twice. The wild horse was too quick and strong, and Aaron had been out of the saddle for too long. His balance was off, and the horse quickly realized that.

With a smile on his kind face, the fifty-four-year-old limped back to me. "I guess I'm not in the shape I used to be in."

He had rolled his ankle, so Aaron stayed out of the saddle and left the training to me, the rookie. The first two days after Smokey learned he could throw off whoever was on his back were arduous. He tried to get me off him, intensely and often. Luckily, I was fit and somehow managed to stay in the saddle. Although Smokey had had one or two humans on his back in the round pen and even packed once into the mountains, he didn't know anything. I had to teach him how to stop, turn, back up, and stand still while I got on and off. Ultimately, I had to teach him to trust me. It was a lot to ask of any horse in two weeks, never mind one who was born wild and had remained wild for so long. Smokey was about seven years old.

As the days passed in Osoyoos, I had to make a hard decision. I began to realize there was no way I would get Coyote ready in time.

He was just too dangerous, too wild. He would put my life and those around me in danger. I really wanted to honor Shaun's life through this ride, but it would have to be done without Coyote. I felt like that horse would hand me the same fate Shaun had been given.

I spoke to Sara about not taking Coyote and she agreed. While we ate Easter dinner at her house, Sara said, "We will find another horse that is broke, and you can take Smokey. Coyote is too dangerous."

Caley had another opinion. Puffing on a cigarette, she said, "You can take him. If something happens to him, it's okay. The desert is full of wildies."

I couldn't believe what this horsewoman, running on extremely high levels of sugar and nicotine, was saying. I loved Caley and am very thankful for all the support and help she offered us during our time in Osoyoos. However, some of the things she said made me cringe.

I tried to get her to understand just how dangerous this Long Ride was, not only for myself and my horses, but also for everyone around us. "Caley, I'm riding next to roads with car traffic. Even if you believe this horse's life is expendable, how about a family driving to Alaska on holidays? What if I lose him, and he ends up flying through their windshield?"

She still couldn't see the danger. The redhead, who had never been farther north than British Columbia, gave me a hard look as she popped open yet another can of Pepsi. "There's lots of room next to the road. You'll be fine. Stop being a sissy."

I gave up trying to have a logical conversation with her and continued to work toward finding a second mount. Luckily, Sara's friend Cole, the horse trainer who was working with Jughead, contacted his good friend Jim McCrae. Jim was a fellow Long Rider, and he agreed to lend me one of his mountain horses. On a sunny Sunday afternoon, Sara, Clara, Aaron, and I drove to Jim's ranch near Princeton, British Columbia. It was a gorgeous property in the middle of the mountains with a large pasture, a creek, a log house, and a few other buildings.

"Welcome to my humble abode." Jim shook my hand with a

strong grip. I liked him right away. Jim was tall and wide like a mighty spruce. He had short, prickly gray hair on his head and face, and dressed and looked like his photo should be next to the word lumber-jack in the dictionary.

We spent a few minutes talking about his ride up the Pacific Coast Trail. It was amazing hearing about his adventures with his two horses and mule in the '80s. "I was the last person to ride that trail north in its entirety without trailering the horses at all," he explained.

After our chat, we caught Mac, a colossal buckskin standing at seventeen hands, and put him into Aaron's stock trailer. Mac was a wild horse from the Penticton Indian Band that Jim had acquired a few years previously. The Long Rider used Mac to pack in the mountains and recently started riding him as well.

"I broke my back a few months ago in an excavator accident and haven't been able to do any riding since. Mac needs the exercise. This will be a great trip for him," Jim said, before giving the horse an emotional goodbye.

The truth is, the Long Rider was lucky to be alive. In his accident, the tree he was knocking over had a bear's den under it. When the tractor flipped over with the tree, the bear was not very happy.

As soon as we arrived at Indian Grove Riding Stables, I saddled Mac and got on him. It was such a relief to get into the saddle and have my horse stand still. I asked him to walk and had him calmly take those first strides. I was so used to the past week of riding the hurricane that was Smokey, fighting to stay on every time he exploded and wondering when the next maelstrom might hit. With Smokey, it took five minutes just to mount him as he tried to run off.

"This horse is amazing," I yelled out to Clara from Mac's back. Being on top of him made me feel as if I was riding an elephant. Not only was he super tall, Mac was also very wide. He definitely had draft blood in him. He made little Smokey, standing at fourteen hands three inches on his tippy toes, look like a pony.

I got off and looked him in his left eye, beautiful light-blue. "Big Mac! That's your new name, buddy!"

Finally, I had a broke horse for my Last Long Ride. This realization made me breathe a little easier that afternoon. However, with only a few days left of training, I still needed to get Smokey as ready as possible and Mac into shape. I wrote to my mom and asked her to please ask my grandma to light one of her candles for us. At this point we needed a miracle.

4

AT A GALLOP

For the rest of my time at Indian Grove Riding Stable, I continued working with Smokey. He got a little better every day, and I started to ride Big Mac. The buckskin had large fat deposits on both sides next to his shoulders. I had never seen anything like it in my life. He was obese, and due to the winter, his coat was a thick and prickly mixture of dark brown and beige. He looked like a shaggy 1970s carpet! I quickly needed to get him into riding shape.

I began going out onto Aaron's trails, riding Mac and ponying Smokey. It was a gorgeous area in the desert, full of sagebrush and flanked by a large lake on one side and a stunning rock-face mountain on the other. It was also plagued with rattlesnakes. On our first ride out, Mac jumped to the right when he neared a sagebrush plant that started to rattle ominously.

At first, I thought a sage grouse had startled him. However, when I inspected the base of the bush, a rattlesnake sat coiled, ready to attack. Luckily, we continued on unhurt. I first started ponying Smokey with just the packsaddle on his back and later with the panniers. The first day I put the panniers on him, he freaked out badly, as expected. He ran circles around me and bucked and tossed his head. Eventually, he realized they weren't going to kill him and calmed down.

On a chilly afternoon, we led the horses into Aaron's trailer and took them to a big open field where the horseman grew hay. For the first time, I would ride Smokey outside of the safety of panels.

"Let's see if you trained this horse or not," Aaron said, sporting a big mischievous grin. He looked like a little kid who just stole candy. I climbed on. I was nervous, but I trusted my little gray was ready. The night before, we had done the same thing, but Aaron had ponied Smokey with me on top.

When we started out, he wanted to run off and wouldn't stop freaking out. After we climbed a steep and long hill, he followed Aaron's big paint horse quietly. I quickly climbed on him with his head facing me, my left rein held tight. While he turned circles, I sat on his back. When I had both feet in the stirrups, I straightened him out and asked him to whoa. I waited for everyone else to get on their horses and we began walking.

"I think we have a broke horse here," Aaron said, looking back at me like a proud father.

I was as proud as he was. This was the first time I worked with a wild horse. Smokey had come a long way from the first day I met him only two weeks earlier.

Eventually, we galloped our horses around the spacious hayfield while I smiled wide. Everything was going well until I looked back and saw that Clara was about to fall off Big Mac. The tall buckskin was spooked by something in the grass and threw her off balance. As she slid down from the saddle at a full gallop, I thought to myself, *Don't get hung up! Don't get hung up!*

Clara hit the grass hard as Mac kept running. I saw everything in slow motion, my heart trying to commit suicide by jumping out of my mouth. Luckily, her foot came out of the stirrup. I got off Smokey and ran to her side. She was stunned. Tears filled her eyes, and she couldn't talk, but after a few minutes we realized she was okay. It was just a scare.

"I got the wind knocked out of me," she said, sitting in the grass.

Smokey passed his test and Clara was unhurt. We were almost ready to start our drive up to Alaska. Maybe my grandma's candle worked.

Riding two wild horses from the Penticton Indian Band and training them in the Osoyoos Indian Band allowed me the opportunity to learn from the elders I met. Aaron Stelkia, Smokey's owner and a master horseman, was the one with whom I spent the most time. While he taught me a lot of tricks about horses, he also helped me understand a bit about his culture and their strong connection with the horse.

"We believe horses were here before the European boats arrived," Aaron told me one day while sitting in his home. To Aaron and many First Nations people, the story that the horse was extinct in the Americas before the explorers arrived does not add up. According to him, his mother Jane Stelkia remembers stories passed down from her ancestors about how horses had always been a part of their lives.

"My mom's DNA traces back to Russia when those people made the trip to the Americas over the land bridge. We think they came with horses," Aaron said. "When the Europeans came across some of the tribes that used horses, they wrote about what good horsemen those Natives were. How could they have learned to capture, train, and ride these animals in such a short period of time?"

His theory is supported by a 2014 study by The Vancouver Foundation, Friends of Nemaiah Valley (FONV), Valhalla Wilderness Society (VWS), and Texas A&M University proving that wild horses in the remote Chilcotin area of British Columbia (600 kilometers Northwest of Osoyoos) share DNA traits with the Yakut horses of Siberia.

At Aaron's mother's house, I got to learn more about this family's strong connection to the horse. At the age of eighty-nine, Jane Stelkia was a strong indigenous woman who had been training horses and ranching since she was a young girl. "Ranching has been in my family for over 100 years," she told me while we sat in her spacious living room. She was petite and seemed extremely fragile at first. However, that illusion faded when I saw her work. She still branded her own cattle and rode. She still possessed great strength.

The curly-haired, dark-skinned rancher explained how important these majestic animals have been to her family and community. "The horse means everything to us," Jane said. "I love these animals, and it makes me proud we still use them to work the ranch today." However, she confessed that in recent years, cowboys were becoming a dying breed. I'd heard the same from all the elderly people I spoke to in the area.

"There are just no more young cowboys anymore," said Thomas Pierre, a cowboy and retired bronc rider in his ranch outside of Penticton. Thomas, who was in his mid-seventies, showed me the arena he built near his home. It was a place where he would allow young kids to get on his more than 100 saddle bronc horses to practice and learn how to ride.

"One day, they just stopped coming, so I sold all of the horses," Thomas told me as he gazed toward the horizon. It was a heavy moment. A silence set in that became hard to lift. It was as if you could hear the thundering hooves of 100 horses running nearby.

I am an eternal optimist, and although at times I shared Jane and Thomas' sentiment, I tried to convince them that there were still cowboys out there, cowboys like me, for instance. Hearing my story, how far I had already ridden and how far I was about to ride on this new adventure, may have given them a little hope. This was my Last Long Ride, but I want to believe I am not the last Long Rider.

While there, I also got to learn a lot about wild horses and their way of life. Listening to Aaron and observing the different herds we came across out in the desert was an unbelievable opportunity. One of the most interesting things I saw out there was the wild studs defecating in the same piles. They created huge mounds of droppings everywhere. They did this as a way to mark their territory, and Smokey continued doing this throughout the entire journey. His aim always blew my mind.

Castrating Smokey and Coyote with Aaron's help, I learned that these horses can have more than two testicles. Coyote, for instance, had two large testicles the size of small footballs, and three smaller ones the size of golf balls that sat higher up. After seeing his five nuts, his behavior and strength began to make more sense. During the castration, Aaron explained his forefathers always taught him to throw the cut testicle past the horse's head so the animal spent his entire life going forward in search of it.

While holding down Coyote's colossal head with all of the strength I had in me, I exclaimed to the master horseman, "Whoa! You almost hit me in the face with that one!"

Aaron simply laughed while he clamped down on the horse's vein to stop the bleeding.

I also learned how each stud has his own group of mares. Younger studs, called bachelors, form their own herds of two or three before gaining the strength and experience to win over their own group of mares. It was all unbelievably cool!

The day before Clara and I drove off to Alaska, Aaron invited us to have dinner with his family to celebrate his son Shaun's life. On that day, five years earlier, the young horseman drowned in Wood Lake.

We visited his son's tomb, made from a mighty tree trunk. Aaron said, "Hey, Shaun! This is Filipe and he is about to go on a big journey with one of our horses. I want you to protect him on this ride."

It was an emotional moment. The wind began to blow uncontrollably with enough force to push me back. I felt like Shaun was there at that moment. I closed my eyes and asked for his protection.

"Nice to meet you, Shaun," I said to the wind.

Aaron had buried his son near the home they used to live in, now burned down, over a rock that Shaun loved to sit on to watch the sunrise. This was where Aaron went as soon as he got home from the hospital the day Shaun passed. "I sat on his rock crying and said a prayer to the Creator and to Shaun. Then I closed my eyes and asked for a sign, any sign, my son had heard me. When I opened my eyes, a crow flew right over my head. I turned around to see the bird, but it was gone. It had disappeared. I couldn't understand, then I looked up and there was the bird, hovering right over my head," Aaron said with tear-filled eyes. "I knew he had heard me."

After we said our prayers, we drove to the same restaurant where we had dinner the first day we met Aaron. His two sisters, their kids, and his mom, Jane, were there. It was a wonderful evening, and before we left, Clara and I took a photo with the family.

"Here. Hold my hand," Jane said, almost making me explode with joy. She held Aaron's hand with her right hand and with her left, in a tight grip, she held mine. At that moment, it was as if they had accepted me into their family.

In her hand, I found my own grandmother's touch. I felt blessed. I knew the candle had worked!

5

THE DRIVE TO ALASKA

I spent so much time working with Smokey and Mac in Osoyoos that the days flew by. The two weeks we were there felt more like two days. It took so much time and effort to get Smokey ready, or kind of ready, for this journey that I didn't get to see any of the tourist attractions in the area. There was the Desert Cultural Centre, Spotted Lake, Rattlesnake Canyon, not to mention the more than fifty wineries in the area. But I wasn't there as a tourist. I was there to begin my Last Long Ride. Although at times it felt like that would be impossible with the cards I was dealt early on, I focused on the job at hand and got it done.

On Monday, April 29, 2019, Clara and I woke up early and began getting our things ready for our big drive.

"I can't believe we are going to Alaska," Clara said while we ate breakfast. We were going in advance of the horses to get things organized, and I was invited to speak at the University of Anchorage on May 3. Sara, Cole, and two other friends from British Columbia would trailer the horses up in a week.

Before we left the stables, I rode Smokey in the early morning to get in one more day of training. Then we said goodbye to the little gray and Mac and gave them some last-minute treats. Finally, we checked the motorhome's oil and the tires. The amazing Marie and Rocky Aitken managed to get the 1990 motorhome through the inspection and drove it out to Osoyoos for us.

Before giving me a strong motherly hug, Marie said, "You guys have a safe trip. Rocky and I will come out at some point to see you two."

Rocky warned us like a dad, "Remember to plan every stage. There's nothing up there."

After saying goodbye to Aaron, Caley, and Jordan and thanking them for their generosity and love, we climbed into our new home on wheels and began the five-day journey. It felt exhilarating. The 3,500-kilometer drive to the final frontier was going to be an adventure of its own.

Clara drove the big vehicle with care. "I remember when we painted the letters in Alaska - Canada on the planning wall before we started scheming more than a year ago," she said. "And now we are on our way there."

On our third day on the road, the motorhome started making a weird sound. It almost sounded like the heater was broken. *Tek, tek, tek!* The noise came from under the hood, fast and not too loud.

"That's not good," Clara said.

I pulled over next to Bijou Falls National Park in British Columbia and opened the hood. Everything looked normal until I checked the oil. It was bone dry.

"This is really not good," Clara said. "It's the pistons we are hearing."

I looked at her with wide eyes. Clarita was the official mechanic in our relationship. We were several hundred kilometers north of Prince George and about an hour from Chetwynd, the next town. We were literally in the middle of nowhere. It was already late in the afternoon. While we contemplated what to do next, a truck pulled over.

"You kids okay?" a tall gentleman in his early fifties asked. We told him about our problem, and he offered to drive us to Chetwynd. Clara and I jumped in alongside his son and another young kid in his early twenties. We made the hour and a half drive north.

When we arrived in the small town, we went to a gas station, and Clara called her seventy-year-old neighbor in Argentina who was an experienced truck driver. Carlitos told us to buy six liters of oil and hope that the motorhome wasn't leaking oil.

"Hopefully, it's just consuming a lot of oil because it's an old vehicle, and it hasn't been used in a while," he said over WhatsApp. We followed his instructions and went back to the highway to try to hitch a ride back to the motorhome. With two plastic bags filled with oil containers in hand, we stood looking into oncoming traffic with thumbs out. It was a long, chilly hour and a half before a miner in a red truck finally stopped and picked us up.

By the time we arrived back at the motorhome, it was dark. I poured the oil into the engine and prayed before turning the vehicle on. Luckily, it started right up, and the engine sounded as smooth as it had when we left Osoyoos. Feeling lucky, we continued north. In just a few hours, we were hit by a major snowstorm that forced us to stop and wait until the next morning to continue. We slept outside of a Tim Hortons that night after a warm bowl of chicken soup.

The farther north we inched along the map of Canada, the colder it got. Aside from the weather, along the way I was able to pinpoint the major obstacles we would meet on our ride south. We saw sixteen bears, four moose, six herds of buffalo, helicopter-sized mosquitoes in the low country, several dangerously narrow mountain passes, and too many long bridges to keep count. Some in the Yukon had a metal-grate deck. It would be quite difficult to get the horses to cross those bridges, maybe even impossible if their hooves could fit through the gaps. But I decided I'd worry about those bridges when I got to them.

On Friday May 3, five minutes before I had to give a motivational talk at the University of Anchorage, we arrived at the Palmer campus. I turned off the motorhome, changed my shirt and went into the building. Pete, a professor at the university and a horse lover who I had been in contact with for a year thanks to the Long Riders Guild, was there to greet me.

"You made it right on time," he said with a big smile.

"I can't believe it. There really is a God," I said.

After making a quick pit stop to pee and brush my teeth, I entered the lecture hall. It was packed with people. I set up my laptop, turned on my presentation, and after a wonderful introduction by Pete's wife Alys, I began telling my story.

THE MORNING after my talk in Palmer, we enjoyed a hearty breakfast at Pete and Alys' house. "You two must be so tired after that long drive," Alys said while we ate fruit with pancakes and homemade yogurt.

Alys was a short, slim writer who wrote a daily blog on her website every day of the year (www.alysculhane.com). She had a PhD in Composition and Rhetoric from the University of Wisconsin-Milwaukee and dreamed of one day becoming a Long Rider (riding more than 1,000 miles consecutively). Alys wore round reading glasses like John Lennon's and had frizzy gray hair down to her shoulders. Eccentric and passionate about horses, she spoke like a hippie from New York City and loved using the catch phrase, "Stranger things have happened."

Alys and Pete lived off-the-grid in a cozy cabin outside of Palmer. It was a beautiful property with several cabins and a large space for their four Icelandic horses. Their electricity came from large solar panels and a generator.

Once we finished our delicious breakfast, Pete announced, "This morning we will go to an event for the Matsu Backcountry Horsemen that we are a part of."

When we arrived at the gorgeous ranch flanked by dramatic snow-capped mountains, I received a beautiful surprise. The Matsu Backcountry Horseman made a $500 donation to the Barretos Children's Cancer Hospital, the Brazilian hospital I raise funds for on my journeys.

Holding the check in my hand, I told the president of the association, "Wow! I will never be able to thank you enough for this!"

Seconds later, I received another donation. "Yesterday, I sold our manure for $150, and I would also like to donate this to the hospital," Alys said before we shared a hug.

"In May 2011, Pete and I traveled in the Rocky Mountains from Gulnare to Vail Colorado by horseback," Alys told me about their epic ride. It didn't amount to 1,000 miles, but they were made "Friends of the Guild." A great start!

After getting to know the members of Matsu Backcountry Horsemen, we went out for a ride on a spacious and dry riverbed. With a stunning and dramatic ridge to our left, we rode down the river enjoying the spectacular view. I rode a little Icelandic pinto, sitting at 12.3 hands. The horse's name was Yokla which means, "She who walks fiercely over glaciers."

Clara rode a tall and kind Rocky Mountain horse named Junior. They looked good together. Yokla and I were a hot mess. She shook her head from side to side, tongue hanging out, prancing on the spot. At one point, she turned her head back and bit the tip of my boot.

"You little rascal! Settle down! I'm not a glacier," I said to her, laughing.

"This is so beautiful, our first ride together in Alaska," Clara said from atop her horse, riding gracefully while I held Yokla back from taking off at a gallop.

Clara towered over me while my feet nearly dragged on the gravel. It was hard to believe we were riding in Alaska together, Clara being from Argentina and myself from Brazil. We'd met on my second Long Ride to the end of the world in the middle of Patagonia. And now to be as far north as possible in the Americas together! This was the girl I wanted to spend the rest of my life with. My *flor del pago*. My soulmate. In my heart I knew our fate was already written by the same hand long ago.

The silver bracelet I had given her in Patagonia, a present from Ramon Bastia's daughter, sparkled around her wrist. Watching the woman of my dreams smile wide with a rugged mountain behind her, I promised myself, "If I make it to Calgary alive, I'm going to ask you to marry me."

After our ride, we went to a small local brewery called Lazy Mountain, owned and operated by a retired pilot, Neil Gotshall. "This was a dream of mine for a long time. Now I can brew my coffee, walk to my own brewery, and start making beer," he said with a big smile over a delicious dinner of Argentinian shrimp (in Clara's honor) at his house. After dinner, Neil, who looked like Bruce Willis' better looking brother, brought out a custom-made wolf fur jacket. It was gray, long, and very warm.

"This jacket keeps you warm even in the coldest Alaska nights," he said with pride as I donned the heavy coat. It made me feel like a rapper!

The following morning was a very special Monday in Palmer: Drive Your Tractor to Work Day! One of the goals of this Last Long Ride was to help preserve and celebrate our western heritage, cultures, and community spirit by celebrating ranchers and farmers. The people who so kindly took me into their homes from Calgary, Alberta to Ushuaia, Argentina, were some of the most hardworking and generous folks I have ever met. They are part of a class who seem to have no worth in the twenty-first century. They feed us three to four times daily, and in return, we as a society blame everything from global warming to rising food prices on them. It was a true blessing to be in Palmer for this extraordinary initiative.

"Farmers are the real stewards of this land, and we need to celebrate and be proud of the work we do," Arthur Keyes, the event's organizer, said. He was a farmer himself. I couldn't agree more with the tall and handsome man.

According to several of the farmers I spoke to that day, the most fertile land in Alaska is found in the Palmer Valley. It's at the Palmer Fair that world-record vegetables can be seen on display every fall.

The 2012 world's record giant cabbage weighed in at 138.25 pounds. This is the average weight for a thirteen-year-old boy! Unfortunately, in recent years farms were being replaced by parking lots and subdivisions in the area.

"We are here today because we want to see a future with thriving local food markets that will give Alaskans access to fresh, healthy food, and keep our farmers farming," Amy Pettit, executive director of the Alaska Farmland Trust Corporation (AFTC), told me.

More than two dozen people participated in the third annual Drive Your Tractor to Work Day. Tractors of all makes, colors, and models took off from Glacier Valley Farm, owned and operated by Keyes. They drove the backroads to downtown Palmer. A delicious, free breakfast of bacon, eggs, potatoes, and pancakes was served in the town hall, everything either grown or produced locally.

Two days later, Amy Pettit took me to visit her brother-in-law Todd Pettit's bison ranch.

"Welcome to my home." Todd gave me a strong handshake. He was a big, brawny man with kind eyes. In his forties, he'd grown up ranching. He was as muscular as a bison bull. His grandfather started this ranch, and when he was a young boy, he spent every moment possible with the elderly gentleman.

"My grandfather was a special man," Todd said. "I learned so much from him." It was difficult losing his childhood hero. Their solid bond was clear by the affectionate way he spoke about his mentor. The ranch, tucked in the midst of tall mountains, was home to about fifty bison. Todd told me several stories about how these big, powerful animals nearly killed him.

"Bison ranching is definitely not for the faint of heart," he laughed. A deep scar from a car accident ran across his wide, pale face. They also used to raise elk at the ranch, but had recently stopped. "Elk are hard to keep fenced in," he said, adding that the bison kept him busy enough.

Amy, originally from coastal Oregon, also grew up ranching. She had long and thick curly hair and warm eyes. Four generations of Amy's family raised premier Black Angus and Angus-cross cattle on their 2,000-acre property. She told me about her work with AFTC. "We want to help farmers continue the legacy that their families have built over generations and generations." It was amazing seeing Todd and Amy's passion for the land and our natural world.

Soon it was time to drive to Fairbanks and organize our departure and the first, very long, stretch of my Last Long Ride.

6

FAIRBANKS

"Anything you need, don't hesitate to ask. Pete and I will see you in Fairbanks soon for the ride out," Alys said before we hugged. Clara and I said goodbye to our kind hosts and from Palmer, Alaska, drove north to Fairbanks.

It was a gorgeous drive that offered a stunning view of Mount Denali (formerly Mount McKinley), the highest mountain peak in North America. With a summit elevation of 20,310 feet above sea level, the top half of the mountain is almost always covered with clouds. It is said that only one out of every three visitors see the mountain in its entirety. We got lucky.

"Wow, that's a gorgeous mountain," I said to Clara while we took photos of the beast.

After studying the mountain for over an hour, we made a stop in Denali National Park. I was so excited to be inside this epic park. It boasted six million acres of wild land that served as home to thirty-nine species of mammals, 169 species of birds, and one lonely species of amphibian. We marveled at the low-elevation taiga forest as it gave way to high alpine tundra, eventually touching the sky through snowy mountains. Being in such an untouched landscape full of beauty and wildlife was an extraordinary opportunity. Unfortunately, we arrived three days before bus tours began in the park.

"This just means we will have to come back to Alaska one day," she told me.

We snapped a photo in front of the iconic "Welcome to Denali" wooden sign. Before settling in Fairbanks, our point of departure for this Long Ride, Clara and I took a drive up to Chena Hot Springs, a gorgeous natural hot spring and lodge situated just north-east of Denali National Park.

"This is the way to rest before a long journey," Clara told me while we soaked in the warm, crystal-clear water. The natural hot spring lake offered a stunning view of the surrounding forest and mountains.

After enjoying our time in the hot water, we turned the temperature down, way down, inside the Aurora Ice Museum. "This is the world's largest year-round ice hotel and bar," our guide said while we put on our very heavy winter jackets. The museum, completed in 2005, stays a cool -7 degrees Celsius all year round. You can visit the ice structure for an apple martini and a tour of the ice sculptures or go all out and spend a night inside, sleeping on an ice bed. With the tips of my fingers frozen and feeling well rested and revitalized from the hot spring, we drove south to Fairbanks. The horses would arrive in a few days, and there was a lot to get done before I started riding south.

We got to Fairbanks three days before the horses did and got to work at once. Our first task was to visit the ranch and boarding stables where the horses would rest before our journey. When I explained my Long Ride to the girl behind the counter, she didn't care much, something I slowly became accustomed to in the north.

After we paid for the horse's stay and made sure it was okay that I started my final ride from the stables, Clara and I went shopping. We were about to journey through some of the most remote areas of North America. We had to have all the equipment, food, and materials we needed for both the horses and ourselves. Once we rode out of Fairbanks, the next major city we would cross was Whitehorse, the capital of the Yukon and 947 kilometers southward. If we forgot something, finding it out in the territory would be nearly impossible.

After making and remaking long lists, we went to war. First, we visited the local tack and feed store, which had a small selection of provisions for horses. We bought items we needed: hoof pick, four bags of hay pellets, three bags of grain, shoeing tools, fly spray, and fly masks for the horses. The list went on and on and on. After spending way too much money — everything was more expensive in Alaska due to hauling distances — we drove to Walmart.

On our second day inside the giant superstore, the final giant cart of materials overflowed with things. As we rang it all up, I complained to Clara, "I hate shopping." (That's right. It took us two days to get everything we needed!)

Since it would take us about two months or more to reach Whitehorse, we needed to stock up on a lot of things. Strategic planning is everything in life. It would mean the difference between success and failure. For this Long Ride, our decisions were a matter of life and death. Lists, planning, and ensuring that nothing was forgotten was critical to my success on the trail. Preparation was almost as important as the ride itself.

Wearing my recently acquired fly mask and holding two cans of bear spray, I declared, "Now, we ride south."

As we celebrated the end of shopping and planning, I looked like a beekeeper. We laughed hard at that.

I AM BLESSED to meet tremendous people who go completely out of their way to help me. Were it not for the kindness of strangers and friends, I never would have ridden a single kilometer, never mind more than 20,000 kilometers! Angels from all over the Americas carried me throughout this nearly impossible dream. Sara Turner is one of those people.

Sara not only rode with me in Honduras and Nicaragua during

my first Long Ride, but she also helped me take care of my beloved horse, Bruiser. On this ride, she connected me to Mac and Smokey, hosted me at her family's home in Penticton, and hauled the horses from Osoyoos, BC, to Fairbanks, Alaska. A 3,315-kilometer trip! Alongside her friends Tara, Max, and Cole, they drove slowly and stopped often to rest the horses.

"What an amazing trip, Filipe! We had so much fun," Sara told me as we drank beer to celebrate the horses' arrival.

"It's so good to see you, Sara! Thank you so much for bringing the boys up," I said to the blonde cowgirl as we shared a long hug.

Sara is one of the most selfless humans I have ever met, a strong woman with a backbone of steel, she gets shit done! When she came back to Canada, she started her own fair-trade coffee shop, Seis Cielo. Honey, her mare, who now lived in Honduras, left quite the mark on her. She was inspired to promote the wild horses that live around her home in Penticton. Too many of these animals were being sold for meat to the slaughterhouses. I was glad we had decided to join forces and use this journey to inspire other riders to give these majestic animals a job, a nice home, and the life they deserve.

When Smokey and Mac came out of the trailer, it looked like they had been hauled from half an hour away. Both horses had lost no weight and held their heads high. Alert, they looked around excitedly. They didn't have a tired bone in them. I couldn't believe it.

"It was six long days, but these boys managed the trip very well," Cole said while we walked them to their pasture for the night. As soon as we set them free in the bright green grass, they took off bucking and galloping. As the sun sank in the distance, it was a beautiful scene. That night, we obviously drank way too much whiskey and beer, as was customary every time Sara and I met.

"I love you, Filipe," Sara said as we walked out of a sketchy basement bar in downtown Fairbanks.

"I love you, too, Sara," I replied, our arms over each other's shoulders like old friends as we laughed. Life is so crazy and mysterious, full of surprises. What were the chances that someone I met in Honduras seven years earlier, originally from Canada, would now be as drunk as a skunk with me in Fairbanks, Alaska? It was the night before I jumped into the saddle for my Last Long Ride, riding two wild horses she helped find.

Everything happens for a reason. Everything was written long ago.

7

SADDLE UP AND RIDE HARD

On Friday, May 17, 2019, I was startled awake in Fairbanks, Alaska. I thought I was late for my own departure. Then, when I saw it was still 6:15 a.m., I realized I was just hungover.

"I hate you, Sara," I whispered before I burst out laughing.

From deep in the blankets on the other side of the bed, Clara protested, "Is it her fault or your fault that you two drink so much when you see each other?"

I didn't have time to solve the world's problems. I needed to get dressed and ready. Today I would start my third and final Long Ride, a realization that made me swallow the little spit left in my dry mouth. I had traveled down this precarious road before. In my other two journeys, I had no idea of what dangers awaited me around the next bend. This time around, I knew exactly how hard this journey would be. It almost seemed like a video game that just kept getting harder and harder at every new level I unlocked. Release metal grate bridges! Territorial moose! Canada's tallest mountains! Massive grizzlies! I would have to pass all these levels while riding two wild horses, and one was a very green and very wild horse. What had I gotten myself into? Again!

I fixed myself a strong coffee, ate a peanut butter and jelly sandwich, and went out to get Mac and Smokey ready. As a thank you gift to Sara, Tara, Max, and Cole for driving the horses up, I found an amazing cowboy family who loaned us horses so they could ride with me for a while.

From atop her stunning dun stud, Johanna Ray said, "Filipe, we are very happy to share this day with you. If it wasn't for horses, we would have never met," She was a blonde Canadian cowgirl from Steinbach, Manitoba, who now lived in Alaska. She wore a beige jean skirt in the saddle and looked like a cowgirl from an old western movie.

Her husband and brother-in-law, who were also there to share this first day with us, were real cowboys in every sense of the word. Both wore leather chaps and carried worn-out ropes tied to their horns. Both team roped and steer wrestled in the rodeos. They arrived early with the extra horses, but unfortunately the gang from Osoyoos missed their alarm. We waited and waited and waited some more, until finally at about 9:30 a.m., they arrived.

"I'm so sorry! I'm still drunk," Sara whispered before letting out a snort. A McDonald's cup, filled with Jack Daniels, dangled from her right hand. Her big, black sunglasses hid her bloodshot eyes. At this point, I was just happy they were alive!

Clara sat astride a majestic Friesian on loan from a friendly teenager so she could ride out with us. Her mount's black hair shone in the midday sun like a freshly polished Lamborghini. The Universe always seemed to put Clara on the flashiest horses around.

As we sat in our saddles for a photo, I looked around at all my friends, new and old from different corners of the globe, who were there for this monumental day in my life. There was Sara, her friend Tara, who is from Ireland, her fiancé, Max, and Cole from British Columbia, all on horses lent by Johanna Ray and her husband John. The Manitoba cowgirl sat atop a muscular Quarter Horse. John and his brother, originally from Oregon, perched atop two quick gray ranch horses. Pete and Alys, originally from California and New York rode their Icelandic horses. An American veteran, once deployed to Desert Storm and Iraq, sat with a wide smile atop her bay mare.

"I can't believe all of these people came to ride out with you! It's amazing," Clarita said from atop her tall steed. Our fingers intertwined.

Were it not for Clara, I don't think I would have taken on this Last Long Ride. Truth is, I had been there and done that. After riding horseback from Canada to Brazil and from Brazil to Ushuaia, I had nothing left to prove to myself or anyone else. On my second journey, the monotony of saddling horses and riding thirty kilometers every day took a real toll on me. My heart wasn't in it anymore. Many days, it felt like any other job, except I was facing solitude, winds of 120 kilometers per hour, and temperatures of -16 Celsius in Patagonia.

After I finished, I thought about retiring from my life as a saddle tramp. Sure, there was an allure when I thought about riding the final stretch from Alaska to Calgary, completing the Americas from North to South. However, records and medals don't mean anything to me. I started my first Long Ride to live out my life's dream. I underwent the second to raise funds for a children's cancer hospital. For this one, the journey couldn't simply be about "finishing the Americas."

This long ride would be a journey of love. I was there thanks to Clara, this unbelievable woman who brought happiness back into my life. She saved me from the loneliness I felt deep in my core before we met. Along with the horse, she helped pull me out of a depression. If I could cheat death one more time, I was determined to drop down on one knee and ask for this Argentinian goddess to spend the rest of her life by my side.

LIKE THE START to all my journeys, there had to be some chaos. As the group of riders made their way out of the horse stables, Pete and Alys, who were green riders on out-of-control Icelandic horses, nearly ran over a family sitting on the lawn.

"Watch out!" was all I managed to yell watching the tragedy about to unfold. Luckily, the mother, in a moment of heroics, scooped up her two kids and dove out of the way. I let out a sigh of relief.

We followed a gravel road next to the Trans-Alaska Pipeline for most of the day. Considered the world's largest pipeline system, it can deliver two million barrels of oil per day.

"This pipeline runs from Prudhoe Bay to Valdez. It's what pays the bills in this state," John Ray said, adjusting his brown felt cowboy hat. He went on to tell me that the United States purchased Alaska from Russia on March 30, 1867, for $7.2 million. That's pennies when you look at the fact that crude oil production in Alaska averaged 448,000 barrels per day in 2020. At $60 a barrel, that's more than $26 million a day. But, of course, the Russians didn't know that then.

The day ended at a boarding facility in North Pole, a small town thirty kilometers south of Fairbanks. In the center of town, tourists visit Santa's house year-round. Apparently, this is where St. Nick calls home, in Alaska, anyway.

Before Sara Turner left for Anchorage to catch a flight home, she gave me the horses' paperwork for crossing the border back into Canada. Along with the paperwork came some troubling news. "Since Smokey and Mac are Canadian horses and in transit in Alaska, you will have to cross the border back into Canada within a month of when their blood was taken for the Coggins exam."

I read through the paperwork. Looking at the date the blood was drawn, May 7, 2019, I counted dates and kilometers in my head. My palms got wet from nervousness. It was May 17. Fairbanks sits 503 kilometers from the Yukon border.

"I have to ride 500 kilometers in twenty days?" Once again, those imaginary lines drawn by men long ago would make my life in the saddle much harder than it needed to be. And, like before, there was nothing I could do but saddle up and ride hard.

IN NORTH POLE, we bid Sara and her selfless entourage goodbye and rested at Sarah Nolan's ranch with her welcoming family.

"I hope you guys like pizza," she said, unloading four boxes of large pizzas from her truck.

"Pizza? I love pizza," I said. That made Clara laugh at the inside joke. (Those who read my second book know how Clara and I met and will understand.)

While we ate the delicious pizza, we got to know this amazing family. They shared why they loved Alaska's lifestyle so much. "We hunt and camp and fish. It's amazing," Sarah's eight-year-old son said with bright eyes. Sarah showed me a picture of a huge black bear she harvested the previous spring.

"You have to hunt them in the spring when they are still eating grass," her husband, a thin man with grease-covered hands, explained. "Later in the year, when they get into the salmon, the meat tastes strong, like fish."

After they shared their story with us, they asked the question everyone wanted to know. Sometimes it came quickly. Other times, it took a few hours of conversing with a family before it arose. But this question was always asked: "How did you and Clara meet?"

This Brazilian cowboy and the Argentinean *gaucha* in Alaska communicated in Spanish, and acted as if we had known each other since forever. "I met Clara on my Long Ride to Ushuaia. I asked to sleep at her family's house and in the morning, stole the farmer's daughter." That made everyone laugh.

"My mother-in-law loves me." That was everyone's favorite line. People loved hearing about how a cowboy met the love of his life in the middle of Patagonia on horseback. In an age where people meet through dating apps, I guess our story did sound a bit like a fairy tale. Only my horse wasn't white, nor was I a prince.

The next morning before we rode out, Clara drove to Fairbanks to pick up Marzio Lorenzo from Globo TV International. The journalist flew to Alaska to capture the beginning of my ride. Alongside Debra and Kathy, two amazing horsewomen who also rode with me on the first day, we headed south.

"We decided to stay for one more day and accompany you today," Debra announced while I tacked up my boys.

This was great news! Not only because I would have company all day, but because Smokey was still extremely green. Having these two experienced horsewomen and their well-trained horses out on the trail made me feel a little safer and more confident. That was, until they started telling me horror stories. Worse yet for me, they were bear stories.

Debra told me the gory story about how one of her friend's horses was attacked and killed by a grizzly. "One time, friends of ours tied their horse to a tree, and when they returned a few hours later, only the head was there." This was not the only bear story I heard that morning! They had an arsenal of grisly stories that they told with vigor as I sank in the saddle with fear.

However, they also offered tips to stay safe on the trail. "You guys will be fine out there. Just be smart, put a bell on the horses at night, and always carry your pepper spray," Kathy advised.

At lunch, I bid them farewell and continued south alone. A few hours later, I found myself in a torrential downpour in front of Eielson Air Force Base. It was a cold rain that came from all sides due to the chaotic wind. While I rode with my hat tilted down to try to protect my face from the rain, both horses took off at a gallop when the airport's loudspeaker went off. Luckily, I managed to stay on, but I couldn't understand what the muffled voice was saying over the speaker. It was too far away, and the rain drowned it out.

"You guys relax now," I said, trying to calm my prancing wild ponies.

It didn't work because as soon as the muffled voice went away, a colossal plane took off right next to us making Mac and Smokey want to run off in the other direction. First, I heard the B-52 Stratofortress' loud turbines fire up like a hurricane getting louder and louder by the second. Then, it screamed down the runway right next to us. The horses completely lost it, with me holding them back with all my strength on the reins and as much confidence as I could muster in my voice. We made it to the other side of the runway alive thinking the fun was over. It wasn't.

A few hours later, I was again trying to stay dry when a fighter jet broke the speed of sound barrier right on top of us. The sonic boom, a large explosion that sounds like a bomb going off, made my heart jump, and my mustangs took off again. I had never heard anything so loud in my life. It sounded like the crackle of lightning, but much stronger. It was like an earthquake in our ears, the kind of noise so deep and powerful you feel it in your soul. My first thought as we galloped along the ditch next to the road was, "The Russians are bombing Alaska!"

We only found out it was an airplane breaking the sound barrier a few days later. I was very relieved. Luckily, that afternoon we arrived at Celebration Ranch. I felt happy to be alive. The horses had freaked out all day at the sonic boom blasting off along with large airplanes landing at and taking off from Eielson Air Force Base. On top of that, right before we rode into the ranch, we crossed paths with a big moose cow and her calf. Like us, they were both drenched from the afternoon's rain.

"Easy now, mama. I'm not here to hurt you or your kid," I said softly from the saddle, praying for the cow not to get angry and charge. Full-grown moose cows can weigh in at 1,000 pounds and stand at five to six and a half feet. They can also be extremely territorial. In Alaska, they injure more people than any other wild mammal, even grizzly bears! An Alaskan later told me moose wound five to ten people in the state each year.

The mama didn't charge us, and thankfully, my wild horses never saw her. Just past 5 p.m., we rode into the ranch. After crossing a burned down house at the entrance, I had to convince my horses the imploded and black home was not going to eat them.

A gentleman in his mid-fifties walked toward us. He had a slight limp, but his youthful smile made him look much younger than his years. "Welcome to Celebration Ranch." Alan Morlan offered me his right hand. The tall man, with a smile like Jack Nicholson loved hockey, and we spent several minutes discussing why the Toronto Maple Leafs, my favorite team, sucked so much. While we chatted, I laughed as I tried to control my nervous horses who had just seen the goats that lived at the ranch for the first time. With flaring nostrils and wide eyes, Smokey stood with his front legs stretched forward and spread apart, looking like he was staring at ghosts not goats. The goats didn't care much about him.

"I don't think your horses have ever seen goats before," Alan said while we laughed at how panic-stricken the horses were. Smokey snorted loudly every couple of seconds. After we fed the boys and turned them out in a muddy, but spacious corral, Alan showed us the horses on the property.

"My wife started with only one. Now I don't even know how many horses we have," he said, shaking his head. A herd of about fifteen, muddy and big, stared at us. After the tour, I thanked Alan for his hospitality, and we went into the motorhome to eat dinner and call it a night.

The next morning, we met Alan's wife and one of his grand-daughters. "The doctors said this little girl would never walk. She was born with cerebral palsy," Alan told me. He held his cute little grand-daughter's hand as she slowly made her way towards the horses. She walked slowly, but she *was* walking. A true miracle. As an incentive, they promised her a pony if she learned to balance herself and walk. She learned and her grandparents kept their promise.

"She just loves riding her pony, and we believe horses have had a strong impact on her balance and ultimately her life," Alan said while the little girl smiled, petting her best friend Peanut.

We accompanied Alan and his family to church that morning before riding out. It was a great opportunity to simply give thanks and ask for protection. After seeing how hard it would be to control my ponies on my second day in the saddle, I sure needed some divine help!

8

ERIC ARRIVES

On day three of my Last Long Ride, Clara and I found refuge in an RV Park.

"I used to have horses back in the lower 48. We would love to host you and your boys," the big fella behind the counter said. For $35, we got a spot to park the motorhome and built our small corral from RG Rural for the horses in the empty parking lot. There must have been over thirty spots with water and electricity hookups for motorhomes and trailers. In a few weeks, it would be full or close to full every night as tourists made their way up the Alaska highway on their summer vacations. Still early in spring, we would be the only ones there that night.

"Okay, I'll be back soon," Clara told me before she drove back to Fairbanks to pick up my childhood friend Eric Forsyth. Eric, one of my best friends from high school, is a professional photographer and loves to travel. He once rode a bicycle with another childhood friend, Mike Heslin, from Bolton, Ontario, to Tofino, British Columbia. When I invited him to travel with us for a part of the journey, it was an easy sell! Eric was also one of my biggest supporters from day one. Before I had any of the sponsorships on my first Long Ride from

Calgary to Brazil, he helped me by taking photos, filming, and putting together a sponsorship package to sell the project.

I waited for about two hours in the empty parking lot as a cold wind blew from the west. The horses grazed on the nearby lawn. I walked around kicking rocks while Smokey and Mac took short steps, their hobbles preventing them from going too far. Just before I was to put them into their corral, figuring Clara and Eric were close to arriving, I decided to let the boys graze a little more by our lot. Holding onto their lead ropes, I let them eat the tall grass patch near a water tap. It was a big mistake. While I held Smokey's lead, he became frightened at a strange noise and shot his head up. The lead went up right where the tap was connected to the white PVC pipe, and in a split second, broke the valve clean off.

"Smokey, you idiot," I muttered furiously while water shot up towards the sky in a strong stream that made both horses want to run off scared. I managed to hold onto both and quickly put them into their corral before figuring out what to do next. The large puddle of water got bigger and bigger by the second. While I searched the property for the main water line, Clara and Eric pulled in.

"So good to see you, brother," Eric said while we shared a tight hug.

"Good to see you, brother. Now help me. We have a problem!"

After having to wake up the old fella who owned the place, we managed to shut off the water. He did not look happy. I promised I would help him fix the tap in the morning and pay for the damage.

Finally relaxing with a cold beer in hand, I asked Eric, "How's Toronto, brother?"

"It's not the same without you," said the tall photographer.

While we got caught up, Eric took his bike out of a large box and reassembled it. We gave his bicycle the nickname Old Wise Gray Horse. When it was finally in one piece, he said, "I can't wait to ride with you tomorrow."

I went to bed that night thinking how lucky I was. In the middle of Alaska, I was sleeping in a motorhome next to the love of my life, while one of my best friends slept down the hall on the dinner table/bed. My two wild horses snored in a compact, portable corral right outside my window. This was a luxurious five-star hotel compared to my first two Long Rides!

MY FIRST MORNING of day four on the road, I shared the journey with Eric and his bicycle. I decided to ride Smokey for the first time. Sure, the half-wild pony had caused havoc the evening prior, breaking a tap and inundating the RV park with water, but it just felt like it was time.

After I fixed the tap with the owner of the RV Park, I warned Eric, "Get your camera ready. We may have a rodeo in a few seconds."

When I stepped into the saddle, my pony trotted around tensely for a few minutes while I turned him left and right. When he seemed to be a little calmer, I asked Clara to pass me Mac's lead rope. This is what worried me the most. *What is he going to do when he feels that lead hit his ass?* I thought to myself.

Clara walked the big horse over. I grabbed the white lead rope, now brown with mud, with my right hand, took a tight grip of the leather reins with my left, and squeezed my legs. Again, Smokey took off at a trot and Mac followed behind. I walked around the lawn for a few seconds before I announced, "It's time."

Without looking back, I aimed Smokey for the RV park's main entrance, holding Mac's lead carefully with my right hand to prevent it from hitting my mount's back end. We were off.

While studying Google maps the previous night, Eric and I saw that there was a shortcut we could take south by following a power line. It cut a path through a forest of spruce trees that ran as straight as an arrow. Since Eric's bike was designed for off-roading, with big fat tires, we decided this would be the best route to follow. Boy, were we wrong! The trail took us up and down giant hills all morning as we climbed a small mountain. We traversed through tall grass and large trees that had fallen over as dinosaur-sized mosquitoes tried to suck pints of blood from our tired and sweaty bodies.

After he finished pushing Old Wise Gray Horse up yet another hill, I told Eric, "It keeps going up, brother. We're screwed!"

"Holy! These mosquitoes are driving me crazy," he said, swatting back and forth with his hands. We pushed on. When we finally got to the end of the trail where it met the Alaska Highway again, we faced yet another problem. We had to get off this mountain down an extremely steep face.

It looked like the equivalent of a double black diamond ski run! As we peered over the edge of this petrifying precipice, Eric asked, "Can the horses make it down?"

"Oh, yeah, these are wild horses, brother. Plus, there is no way I'm riding ten kilometers back to where we started." We began fighting our way down. I walked, falling over and over again next to Mac. I let Smokey do his own maneuvering down the steep mountain. We slowly snaked our way down, zigzagging from one side to the other.

"Shit, I just ripped my legs apart," Eric yelled after one of his many falls. Finally at the bottom, after about thirty minutes, we let the ponies graze while we looked up in awe. We were sweaty, itchy, and tired. Our legs were scratched up and bleeding to the point they looked like an angry herd of cats had clawed them to bits.

"Welcome to Journey America," I said to Eric. At that, we both burst out laughing.

Smokey did great for his first day! Climbing that mountain, far away from the car traffic on the highway, was a huge help. Although the terrain was difficult to navigate, it was the perfect place for him to start. Eric's bike also helped give the inexperienced mustang some confidence. Both Mac and Smokey believed Eric was also riding a horse and would follow him over bridges and any other obstacles that scared them.

The bike earned its nickname for its extraordinary ability to convince the horses to cross bridges that they didn't want to! Mac and Smokey followed the photographer over a small bridge. They had refused to cross it seconds earlier due to the change in color in the asphalt.

"Just follow Old Wise Gray Horse, boys...no need to fear," Eric joked.

IT WAS a beautiful Alaskan sunny night in late May. The sun was up nearly twenty-four hours a day when we found a great place to camp next to Mount Denali. While we enjoyed the view of the colossal mountain glowing before us, I murmured, "This will be a beautiful river to spend the night by."

Ever the professional photographer, Eric took the opportunity to capture some stunning images of the horses and me before we assembled the small green corral we carried. We gave the boys water and hay, and after a delicious dinner, we went to bed.

All of a sudden, I was awoken by a loud, piercing thump.

Eric yelled, "Mac just jumped out of the corral!"

Still half asleep, I had no idea what he was talking about. Clara ran outside. Under an Alaskan sky still burning bright at 1 a.m., she spotted Big Mac heading toward the road. Tired of being pushed around by Smokey in the small portable corral, the towering horse took a leap of faith. The five-foot-tall panel he jumped over was badly bent but surprisingly did not break. Luckily, Big Mac was unhurt.

Eric told us over breakfast the next morning, "I heard this terrible noise, and when I looked out the window of the motorhome, Mac was dragging his back legs off of the top of the green panel."

But Mac wasn't the only one trying to run away in Alaska. On a cool afternoon, a few days later, while I enjoyed the stunning view around me, Smokey blew up. In survival mode, I leaned back, tightened my thighs into the pommel of my saddle and reached for the horn. Smokey was in full bucking mode due to the cloud of horseflies around his head. After he bucked for about five seconds, I managed to turn his head to the left by pulling on the reins and got him into a controlled lope. I finally stopped him. Mac, on the lead behind us, let out a big disapproving snort.

"Please don't ever do that again," I warned Smokey as a transport truck raced past us on the highway a few feet away.

Riding the Alaska Highway proved to be much more difficult than I ever imagined. Unfortunately, the north is so boggy, this was the only road one can follow south. Due to the muskeg, there are few trails, and none that run north to south. The ones that exist only really open in mid-summer due to the amount of snow up on the mountains. Next to the highway built of logs and gravel to contain the muskeg, there is also not a lot of room. We had about ten meters from the highway on each side, and in many places, it was too easy to sink. The only hard ground was the shoulder immediately next to the road. In the first few days I realized how dangerous this ride would be. We would have to follow the Alaska Highway for eighty percent of this journey.

Since there was no other way but to ride on, I put the horses' fly masks on and continued trekking towards the Canadian border.

AFTER SIX LONG days on the road, we arrived in Delta Junction, our first resting point on our Last Long Ride. Looking down the barrel of the camera while the horses rolled behind me, I announced, "I'm so happy to have just covered the first 160 kilometers."

Luckily, we found a great place for them to rest in the town's rodeo grounds. Brittany, the young lady who ran the grounds, waived the fee for the horses' stay. "You don't have to pay us anything, Filipe. We love what you are doing. We will also bring your boys a bale of hay in the afternoon."

I introduced her kids to Mac and Smokey. They loved them right away. Both wanted to ride Big Mac but were too afraid to actually get on. I offered to throw her cute little nine-year-old boy up on the horse, but he declined. "I'm too little to ride him."

I simply agreed with him and thanked Brittany for her generosity. I couldn't believe our luck! To top it off, my friends Arnon Melo, Peter

Hawkins, and Naira Schiavon, who had been instrumental to my journeys, flew to Alaska to see us.

"We are so excited to spend a few days with you guys." Peter wore his hood over his head due to the mosquitoes. "I told you I hate mosquitoes, right?" he added miserably.

When we arrived at their hotel, Arnon, always energetic and peppy, asked, "What do you guys need? We are here to help and make your life easier."

Peter and Arnon were my first sponsors ever. When I was looking for support for Journey America Part I, their company, MELLOHAWK Logistics, jumped on board before I had the saddles, cameras, or the horses. They truly believed in my dream.

While I was still in university and working on the strategic planning of the first ride in Toronto in late 2010, Peter handed me an envelope of money. "Hopefully, this will help kick-start your project, Filipe."

I can't even begin to explain how much power his words and support gave my crazy project. Very few people believed I would be able to undertake this impossible journey. He and Arnon, two very successful entrepreneurs, turned that tide. Throughout my ride through the Americas, they continued to support me and the project, even flying to Barretos, Brazil for the grand finale of the first long ride. Peter has also been instrumental in all my books and became a mentor in my life. He is an extraordinary writer, editor, and friend. Naira, a long-time friend of Peter and Arnon, had become a new friend of mine. The Air Canada employee was the one who moved Clara and me up to first-class when we flew to Toronto.

We spent an amazing two days in Delta Junction drinking, eating, and laughing with these amazing friends. It was so nice having so many familiar faces around me, so much love. This was such a contrast to my other journeys where I was usually alone amid strangers and thousands of kilometers away from those I love. When you have good friends around you, you have everything!

After a few days off, I felt ready to tackle the next portion of the journey: 173 kilometers from Delta Junction to Tok.

9

ROAD TO TOK

Our ride from Delta Junction to Tok began with a near catastrophe. After crossing a long bridge with the help of Eric and his Old Wise Gray Horse, Clara gave me some terrible news. "Something exploded under the hood of the motorhome, and now there's a liquid leaking."

I couldn't believe our bad luck. Only on the second week of the journey and we were already facing problems with our support vehicle. I tied up the horses to some nearby trees and went about inspecting the motorhome.

"Wow! The battery exploded," Eric exclaimed as soon as we looked under the hood. The black battery glaring back at us had a hole the size of a golf ball on the top right side. As luck would have it, an elderly couple who were driving their truck and trailer up to Alaska stopped to take photos of the horses and me. They had met Sara, Cole, Tara, and Max in British Columbia a month before when they were trailering the wild horses to Alaska. They told the couple my story, and the two couldn't believe they were now meeting us in person.

"This is so cool. Is there anything you need?" the kind lady asked while Eric and I tried to figure out what to do next.

"Well, yes. Can you please give me a ride to Delta Junction?" I asked.

They cleared some room in their back seat, and sitting next to their snappy poodle, I learned all about their trip. They had retired recently and now spent their summers traveling the United States in their brand new truck and trailer. They would spend their winters in Mexico with their three grandchildren. After about half an hour, we were like old friends. They dropped me off at a NAPA store, and I hugged them goodbye.

I went inside hoping this place would help solve my problem. I bought a new battery from a kind brunette with a Texan accent and got a list of the local mechanics. "Not sure anyone will go out there today," she said with her thick, drawn-out accent. "It's Saturday of a long weekend, but it's worth a try. Good luck!"

I walked across the street to a gas station, bought a strong coffee, and sat on the ground outside with my new battery and list of phone numbers written on a piece of cardboard. The first name on the paper was John Parson. It sounded like a character out of a murder mystery novel. I dialed the number next to his name and spoke to the old mechanic. Surprisingly, he agreed to pick me up in his Oldsmobile and drive out to the motorhome. "Don't worry, kid. If there's something wrong with that alternator, we may be in trouble, but let's hope it's just a leak in the battery that caused it to explode."

John seemed like he was from a different era. The elderly fellow had a long white beard like the Oak Ridge Boys. He wore denim overalls and spoke Mid-Atlantic English like he was in a 1930s black and white film. Thankfully, they had batteries in the 1930s. John knew his stuff. With one quick look at the hole in the battery, the mechanic said, "Yup! The old battery was leaking fluid, and a spark set it off."

We took out the old battery, replaced it with the new one, and after hooking the cables up and paying John $100, we were off once again into a long stretch of nothing. Clara and Eric took turns riding the bike next to me. That made the days go by much, much quicker.

We heard nearby wolves howling one night. It was a majestic sound that was both enchanting and petrifying to listen to.

On one of our nights on the trail, we slept on the shores of Moon Lake. With the setting sun kissing the cold water with its powerful globe of fire, we took in the magical scene. Four trumpeter swans made the evening even more beautiful as they took off and landed on the lake. These white birds have a black beak and are impressively large. Males average over twenty-six pounds, making them North America's heaviest flying bird. To get that much mass aloft, the swans need at least a 100-meter-long runway of open water. Running hard across the surface, they almost sounded like galloping horses as they generated speed for take off. Their characteristic deep, trumpeting, "Oh-OH" call also added to nature's soundtrack. It was an unforgettable night!

After six long days on the road, we finally made it to the outskirts of Tok! Not pronounced like the Tok on TikTok, but "Touk." As we neared the small town of 1,258 people, Eric, Clara, and I made plans about what we would eat that night at Fast Eddy's, the local diner. The list was long, but first, we needed to find a place for the ponies.

In the far north, locating a temporary home for the horses to rest was near impossible. Due to the ubiquitous muskeg, there are very few farms or ranches. Luckily, while looking online, we found a B&B for humans and horses. When we arrived, a big woman with short gray hair named Betty Solbeski welcomed us with a warm smile, generosity, and love.

"You guys can stay in my cabins while you're here, no need to pay anything and please take as much hay as you need from the barn," the kind lady in her seventies said. Betty and her husband had built this horse-friendly B&B thirty years previously. It had large corrals, a barn, and two cute wooden cabins. Catering to the Americans hauling horses to Alaska for the summer from the lower 48, it was the perfect place to rest and get ready for our final push to the Yukon border.

"I don't know how we will ever be able to thank you! Please let us know if we can do any chores around the place," Eric offered.

"Well, there actually are some things you two strong boys can help me with," she said shyly. Betty had lost her husband just a couple of years before. She spoke about him, her immense love very apparent, and at the end, shed some tears. It was clear she was still dealing with her loss and learning how to continue life without her partner.

"We are here to help. Whatever you need just let us know," I said.

Betty showed us some trees she wanted cut, boards that needed new nails on the cabins, and a few other small projects. With cold beer nearby, Eric and I happily got to work.

After we were done, Eric packed up Old Wise Gray Horse, and we went to town for our final dinner together. The next morning, he would take a bus to Anchorage where he had rented a van to explore the coast for a couple of days before his flight back home to Toronto.

Toasting Eric, I said, "It's been so nice having you out here, brother. Thank you so much for coming out and taking such beautiful photos."

"It was amazing. Thank you guys for having me," he responded before we both took a long gulp of beer.

ON OUR FIRST night out of Tok, camping next to the road, Betty drove the thirty kilometers south to bring us dinner. "I hope you two like salmon," she announced, holding two plates in her hands.

With a smile on her pretty face, Clara replied, "I love salmon."

By this point, Clara had learned an important life lesson in the cultural differences between Latin America and North America. Where we're from, Brazil and Argentina, when someone offers you something like a plate of salmon, first you say, "No, thank you." The person offering you the delicious treat will then continue to offer it until you ultimately say, "Okay, I'll try some, thank you." This is the polite way to accept something back home.

In the United States and Canada, people will offer you something once. If you want it, then you say yes. If you don't, you say no. It's simple. No dilly-dallying. It's much easier than beating around the bush like we do in Latin America.

"Damn, I really wanted to try that pie," Clara confided to me once while we were training the horses in Osoyoos. She had said no, thinking the person was going to continue offering a piece of the delicious dessert. However, in good old Canadian fashion, the first no was taken to heart, and the pie was put away. Luckily, Clara was a quick learner!

"This salmon is delicious, Betty. Thank you," she said while we dug into the pink fish and colorful vegetables. We ate dinner together that night, talking about life and the road ahead.

Before she left, Betty gave us one more present. Or better, two! She passed me two thick and heavy horse blankets. "I brought my horses' old blankets for your boys. I know it's summer, but we've had snow every month of the year here in Alaska."

"Wow, thank you so much for this," I said, taking the blankets from her. I couldn't imagine I would actually need to use them in the middle of the summer. Boy, would I be proven wrong in a few weeks! Betty was another angel put in our path.

With our time quickly winding down to be in the United States legally with the horses, we had to ride nonstop from Tok to the border — 180 kilometers. If we did so, we would arrive at the Canadian border on the final day of our in-transit permit — day twenty since leaving Fairbanks.

It was a stunning ride south. Flanked by dramatic snow-capped mountains, we encountered one junction that had a gas station and that was it. The rest of the time we were in no man's land. We camped on the side of the Alaska Highway with the horses high lined every night.

Some days we put up the corral. However, after Mac jumped out, we were afraid of leaving both horses inside together. Instead, we would high line one and let the other roam free in the corral, alternating every couple of hours. We also put a cowbell on Mac's neck every night to alert us if something happened. If the bell started ringing frenetically, we knew he was out or there was an animal in camp. It also helped to keep bears at bay. They can be very curious animals, but when they hear a noise they don't recognize, they usually respect it and stay away.

During this stretch, I was forced to use Vaseline on Mac's back to prevent the saddle pad from chafing him. Due to our quick pace to get to the Canadian border before the horses' in-transit permit expired, the hairs on the big buckskin's back were starting to rub away. Every day before I saddled him using a special foam pad I learned to make thanks to Brazilian Long Rider Pedro Luis de Aguiar, I would rub Vaseline where the friction from the pad was starting to irritate Mac. I would re-apply the smooth gunk three times a day or more. "This stuff is a true miracle," I said to Clara after I finished the first pot of Vaseline.

Before we made it to the border, we met two extraordinary women from different corners of the globe only a few kilometers apart. At the Tetlin National Wildlife Refuge Visitor Center, we met Cora Demit. She was a dark-skinned lady in her early sixties who wore thick reading glasses. A proud Athabaskan lady, she knew her language, traditional songs, and took part in all cultural activities. Cora told us about the rich culture of the Athabaskan people who inhabited this region for thousands of years.

"Growing up, we just lived on caribou, berries, roots, fish, and such. I had no house dwelling, strictly canvas tents. By sharing my story with people like you from around the world, I want to ensure my culture does not die."

We thanked Cora and before we left, she offered a prayer to keep the horses and me safe. To Clara, she gave a beading kit to make a fireweed flower on a square piece of leather.

"Oh, my goodness, thank you so much for this," Clara said, examining her new gift with pride.

Only three kilometers south, I was stopped by Myrian, a Brazilian woman, and her American husband. "We just visited the Tetlin Visitor Centre and saw in the signature book that someone had just signed from Brazil. I asked the lady, and she told me you were traveling on horseback, so we had to meet you."

Myrian and I shared a long hug. It's not every day you meet a fellow countrywoman in Alaska. With her husband (another Eric and a retired pilot) they were visiting all sixty-three national parks in the United States. The inside of their Mercedes van looked like a modern New York apartment, complete with a couch, kitchen, shower, and bedroom.

"We have already visited forty-three," the tall brunette said with pride. The idea to visit national parks came after a major scare. In 2009, Myrian had been diagnosed with breast cancer. The experience changed her life. "While I was still recovering from the first surgery, I told Eric, 'All those things we thought we are going to do one day, that one day is now.'"

We bid Eric and Myrian goodbye and continued south in the solitude of the Alaska Highway, pushing for the Medicine Line.

"I have no idea how you always manage to arrive right on time," Clara said while I drank a gulp of Pendleton whiskey to celebrate my arrival at the Yukon border.

"Me, neither," I replied before taking another drink. We talked about how I arrived in Barretos for the first Saturday of the rodeo back in 2014, having left from Calgary, Alberta more than two years prior. I'd made it to Ushuaia exactly on the day I said I would arrive. People came to celebrate with me from all over the Americas and attended a reception put on by the mayor.

For someone who travels at three to four kilometers per hour and thirty kilometers a day on horseback, I really don't understand how I manage to meet dates like I do. It's especially dicey when horses can get hurt, anytime and anywhere. I think it's God's work. Or the Universe. Or my attention to planning. Maybe it's a combination of the three!

It was day nineteen of our ride, and we were camping at an old, abandoned gas station less than one kilometer from the American border office. Down a small hill, we could see the building in the distance. The large cement structure had a pale blue roof and a large American flag waving in the wind. I could hardly believe it. The next morning, day six on the road from Tok, I rode the final kilometer to the US border. When I arrived at the large gray building, I stepped off of Smokey and tied the gray next to Mac on a brown metal railing. I walked into the building with my passport and the horses' papers in hand. A colossal grizzly bear pelt hung on the wall behind the immigration desk.

When I handed the US immigration officer the papers, he looked up at me with confusion. "What do I do with these?" the officer asked me.

I couldn't believe it. I had just ridden 470 kilometers in twenty days to arrive on the final day of our allowed time to transit through Alaska with the horses, and he was asking *me* what to do with the papers? I was astonished.

"I don't know. Stamp it and send a copy to your federal vet maybe," I said in a tone much harsher than I had intended.

He did just that, and in five minutes, we were on our way. I was excited to be officially out of the US, but in order to actually enter Canada, I still had to ride thirty kilometers to the Canadian border office. It was bittersweet. But first, we had to take photos and film at the bright yellow Alaska and dark blue Yukon signs. It was surreal standing there next to those signs with my two wild horses and Clara.

"How did we all get here?" I asked Clara. We had no answers, but to me we were simply going through the motions following our destinies. What were the chances these four beings from totally different places in the globe would meet and be at the Canadian-Alaskan border at that exact moment? On a journey from Fairbanks to Calgary? It was simply meant to be!

Halfway into our day, Clara saw the first bear of the journey. A young male grizzly walked around a trash can at a rest area. Luckily, by the time I rode by with the horses, he was gone.

Later, safely inside the motorhome, Clara regarded me with worried eyes. "He wasn't very big, but I'm so scared for you and the horses, Filipe! Do you have your pepper spray? Please be careful!"

She was petrified of the bears and couldn't understand how I managed to stay cool knowing I was exposed to such dangerous animals all day. There was no place to hide if one attacked. Truth is, I also worried for my safety, but when you have faced as much adversity and danger as I have in my life, fear just doesn't mean the same thing as it does to normal people.

Throughout my life, I have been able to train my mind to block out the fear sensor in my brain. Fear is as old as life on Earth. It is what kept us safe when we inhabited caves and stumbled upon bears and tigers on a daily basis. However, as my father used to tell me when I was little, "Fear is simply a monster that inhabits our minds. If we can't put that monster aside and silence it, we will never live out our dreams."

The adrenaline fear gives me is the fuel I use to overcome obstacles. Sometimes, that fuel runs out. Only five kilometers before officially entering Canada, I almost fainted. I was exhausted beyond belief from the past few weeks and in terrible pain. To top it off, summer was now in full swing, and the sun was cooking my brain.

"I just need to lie down for a sec," I told Clara. She looked worried. After fifteen minutes resting in the shade and drinking a lot of water, I continued on. Clara went ahead of me and parked the motorhome about 500 metres from the border where we had our final meeting.

"Okay, this is the last border we will cross. You know how much I hate borders and how much they hate me. Let's not bring any more attention than we have to ourselves," I said in a worried tone.

She agreed. We kissed and she was off toward the lifeless buildings in the middle of the wild Yukon. I watched her inch away slowly in the old motorhome as I begged the heavens for this last border crossing to be painless.

In the distance, Clara parked the motorhome in front of the border. After a few seconds, a loud siren screamed in the distance, followed by an immigration officer running towards her.

Oh, no! What did I do? she thought to herself.

Actually, he was super nice. He was Canadian and just said she couldn't park there. She drove up to the lineup of cars and waited to cross the border while I watched.

However, I didn't know what was going on. I murmured to

Smokey and Mac, "I thought I told her not to bring attention to ourselves. I don't think she understood me, kids."

After about five minutes, I arrived at the border and rode up next to the motorhome, now in the correct line that would take us to a drive-thru style window.

"I parked in the wrong spot," Clara explained with a nervous smile.

"I saw," I shot back, my usual border-panic taking me over. When the car in front of us drove into Canada, I walked the boys ahead and Clara slowly drove next to us.

"So, you're the horse guy," the kind officer said when I showed up to the window with Mac and Smokey.

"Yes, sir," I replied with a wide smile and puppy dog eyes. I tried to make myself seem like anything but a threat to this great nation. The officer stood next to a young woman who had a thick French accent. I quickly realized he was training her.

"Okay, take the passports and the papers he has for the horses," he instructed her as she repeated the orders received from her workmate.

"Yes, ma'am. Here they are," I said, giving her my passport and the horses' Coggins test results.

I felt terrible that this poor woman was about to get the test of her life on her first day on the job! I was giving her the worst-case scenario. A Brazilian immigrant with "history" in Canada, traveling with an Italian passport (my grandfather was Italian) walks up to the Yukon border with two wild horses. At least she would never again face such a complicated situation in her career.

She took the deep-red passport first and scanned it on her computer. I knew what was about to happen. It was like watching someone get on a horse you know is going to buck. I cringed as I waited for her reaction. It was both nerve-racking and exhilarating.

Wide-eyed, the young immigration officer looked to her instructor. "Um, what do I do now?"

"Let me see this," he said to his colleague, scooting over so he was in front of the computer. Pressing the down button on his keyboard, he began to read my very, very long file.

He said the words I had become so accustomed to hearing. Every time I tried to enter the Great White North, the script was the same. "What did you do in Canada?"

I began to tell the same story which had haunted me since I was a kid (and I emphasized the word *kid*). "When I was a kid, my dad had a work permit. Eventually, he applied to stay in Canada for humanitarian reasons. His request was denied."

The officer gave me the horses' papers back. "Okay, I need to talk to my superior. Can you please wait by the airport up there to the right?"

Clara had no problems entering. Before we walked over to the airport across the highway, Mac rolled in the neatly trimmed grass by the window. In the line of several cars and motorhomes that sat behind us waiting, tourists took out their phones for a photo.

"This is the show while you wait," I said. "Welcome to Canada!"

We waited by the Beaver Creek airport while they studied my passport and my story. This was the first time my waiting room had a pasture for my horses to eat! It was also the first time I entered Canada on horseback for that matter. Every other time, I waited in a tense immigration room at Pearson Airport in Toronto filled with people speaking different languages awaiting our fate. It usually took about fifteen to twenty minutes for the officers to realize that I wasn't lying or doing something wrong. My family went back to Brazil when we were told to. I returned with a student visa after that, finished university, and had entered and left the country several times as a tourist since.

There was one time it didn't go quite so well! It was the first time I returned to Canada after my Long Ride to Ushuaia. One of my childhood friends, Derrick Nield, was getting married to the love of his life. I was so excited for him and to see all of my friends. Since I filmed my journeys for NC2 Media, the production company that sponsored all of my journeys, I had all of their filming equipment with me. I couldn't FedEx the black Pelican Case filled with video cameras, cards, lights, and mics back to the Tennessee-based company from South America. Instead, they asked me to ship it from Canada the next time I flew up.

"How many bags do you have?" a sour immigration officer asked.

"I have two checked bags and a carry-on, ma'am," I replied.

"And you are here for only two weeks? Why so much luggage? What's the reason for your visit?"

I told her about Derrick's wedding first and then explained that only one checked bag carried my clothing. The other was the black Pelican Case with the equipment from NC2 Media. When I finished telling her about my trip, she asked if there was someone who could confirm that I was in Canada for a wedding.

"Yes, of course. My friend Mark Maw is here to pick me up. I'll call him." I explained to him I was in immigration, and that the officer wanted to confirm I was in fact here to attend a wedding. He said okay and I passed her the phone. What happened next was straight out of a movie.

"Hello sir, I just want to confirm that your friend is here in Canada to take photos of your friend's wedding, correct?" she demanded.

I looked at her completely and utterly in shock.

While she listened to Mark's answer and paid no attention to me, I asked, "What are you talking about?"

"Okay, perfect," she said. "And how much will he get paid for his work?"

Again, I tried to protest these ridiculous questions with no luck. Mark, who knew how much hassle I got trying to enter Canada every time, was doing what any other friend would do. He was vouching for me. Due to the way she posed her questions, she made him believe that in order for me to enter the country, I had lied to her that I was coming to work. With no real immigration knowledge, Mark fell for her trap. "Um, he's getting paid $500 dollars."

My best friend later told me how nervous he was when she asked the question. He just said the first number that came to his mind.

"Okay, thank you sir," the immigration officer said before hanging up the phone and passing it back to me. My jaw was on the floor next to my boots at this point. I was livid.

"You're crazy, lady! First of all, I don't even have a camera to take photos in that Pelican Case! Like I told you, it's filming equipment, and secondly, you trapped him into lying based on the way you asked him these questions! You can't do that!"

My assertive tone made me regret my words as soon as they came out of my mouth. I knew the angrier I became, the worse the situation would become for me. However, there's only so much punching one can take. I had been taking blows from these navy-blue uniformed folks since I was sixteen years old. I was tired of being a punching bag, and my patience had run out.

"I can do whatever I want, Mr. Leite. You are not entering Canada!"

I yelled back, "Open the Pelican Case! Please, I implore you. You have just created a story that doesn't exist. This is ridiculous!"

"Go sit down over there, and wait for me to call you." She turned around and walked into a back room with my passport. Shaking my head and laughing to myself at the situation, I made my way to the metal chairs. Immigrants from India, Mexico, and other parts of the world sat there waiting for their verdicts while babies cried and elderly ladies prayed.

Being an immigrant teaches you many things, but the most important lesson one learns from run-ins such as this is being able to face ridicule and to maintain humility. You will be ripped apart. You will be judged. You will be treated like a criminal. You will be humiliated.

After what seemed like a lifetime, the lady returned to her computer and without looking up called my name. Her tone was still stoked with anger, but her voice was lower. I made my way back to her.

"You got lucky today, Mr. Leite," she said, stamping my passport.

"Lucky, lucky, you're crazy, lady. I am not doing anything wrong. You created something in your head that's not real."

She threw my passport at me, and I stormed off, still calling her crazy.

"I'm going to make a note in your file, Mr. Leite," she yelled after me.

Now, a few years later, here I was, once again, awaiting my fate at the Canadian border. At least the view in the wide-open Yukon was nicer than the stuffy immigration office at Pearson Airport.

After about ten minutes, the officer walked over with my stamped passport. "Welcome to Canada, guys," he said with a big smile. "Sorry you had to wait here so long."

Surprised at how kind and polite he was, I replied, "Thank you, sir."

"I think what you guys are doing is super cool," he added. After we snapped a selfie with the excited officer, I rode the final kilometers into Beaver Creek.

It felt good to be back in Canada. It felt great to be 500 kilometers south from Fairbanks. What felt best was knowing that after crossing fourteen international borders with horses, suffering every time, this was the final one I would cross. Altogether, I had traveled over the US - Canada border, US - Mexico, Mexico - Guatemala, Guatemala - Honduras, Honduras - Nicaragua, Nicaragua - Costa Rica, Costa Rica - Peru, Peru - Bolivia, Bolivia - Brazil, Brazil - Uruguay, Uruguay - Argentina, Argentina - Chile, Chile back to Argentina (Tierra del Fuego), and now finally Alaska - Canada. If you think it's a long list to read, imagine having to cross all those arbitrary lines with horses! All the bureaucracy, paperwork, money, diplomacy, stress, and patience it took nearly made me want to pull my hair out.

Clara and I ate dinner that night at the one and only restaurant in Beaver Creek. "Now we celebrate and rest before taking on the land of the midnight sun," I told her.

10

LAND OF THE MIDNIGHT SUN

One month before arriving in Beaver Creek on horseback, we drove through the small border town en route to Anchorage. There was a terrible snowstorm that day. We stopped at the Beaver Creek RV Park and Motel gas station to ask if we could leave four bags of hay cubes and two bales of hay for the horses. We'd bought the feed in Yukon's capital, Whitehorse. We bought the hay from Karen Hardy before leaving Osoyoos. Since there would be no place to buy hay or feed until we arrived in Whitehorse, about two months into the ride, we had to drop it off strategically in order to feed the horses during the arduous journey.

Inside the warm gas station variety store, Beat Ledergerber said, "Yes, you can leave it (hay and feed) in our shop, no problem." The gentle elderly fellow with hair the color of snow had a hard time hearing what I said. However, with his warm and kind smile, we figured it out. I stashed the hay and bags of pellets in his shop with the help of a local police officer, and we continued on to the Alaskan border.

As I rode into the small town of eighty people on Smokey, ponying Mac, I searched the horizon for Beat's RV Park. Canada's most westerly city looked a lot different now that winter's blanket of snow had lifted and given way to the bright green grass of summer.

Before I even reached the park, the elderly gentleman, originally from Switzerland, parked his old Barney-purple truck on the side of the road to welcome us.

"You made it, my friend! Well done! We are waiting for you and your horses at the RV Park," Beat said with a smile. He gave Smokey a hug around his neck and a kiss. He reminded me of Popeye the Sailor Man. We rested with Beat and his wonderful wife Jyl Wingert at the RV Park for three days. "You guys don't need to pay us anything," Jyl said the first day we arrived. After all the riding we had just done, it felt heavenly.

During our stay, we heard stories of bears entering homes at night and the ravens that followed Beat's truck back and forth several times a day.

"We used to host 300 tourists a night during the summers for twenty-two years, but one day the buses stopped coming," Beat said with a sad look.

For years, large motor coaches used to bring thousands of tourists from Whitehorse through Beaver Creek on their journeys to Alaska every summer. But with flights getting cheaper and the switch to boat cruises and motorhomes in recent years, the buses stopped running in such large numbers putting the Rendezvous Dinner Show to an end.

Before we watched a DVD of the performance, Jyl said, "They (tourists) used to love the show. It's so sad that it had to end."

My favorite song from the musical was an original called "301 Miles from Nowhere." It referred to the distance from Fairbanks and offered a welcome tune to visitors.

I couldn't believe how good the show and the songs actually were! With talent good enough for Broadway, actors sang songs about the Yukon's wilderness, its wildlife, and rich history. Suddenly, an airplane comes crashing partway through the ceiling above the fire pit, and a disheveled bush pilot shinnies down a knotted rope into the middle of the room. The crowd goes crazy laughing. It's amazing!

In the large circular building Beat built especially for the performances, one lonely piano sat on the stage. As I looked around, imagining the performances I had seen on the DVD, I heard a tune. For a second, I thought it was coming from my mind, but when I looked at the piano, it was the RV park owner rocking out.

"Wow! You're amazing," I said to him when he stopped. "Keep going!"

"No, no, that's it," he said in his thick Swedish accent before closing the piano keys and walking off the stage with an unlit cigar stuck in the side of his mouth.

During our time in Beaver Creek, we also discovered an extraordinary museum built by a Dutch Canadian named Sid Van der Meer. He had six antique cars in his collection, army trucks from the construction of the Alaska Highway, a full barber shop from the early 1900s, the old airplane that was used to crash into Beat's show, and a turtle fossil that's more than 37 million years old.

"I just can't pick a favorite item," said Van der Meer, standing in the middle of the Old West bathhouse section of his museum. Sid, who learned English by reading the book *Renegades* by Roy Rogers over and over again when he first arrived in Canada, worked at the tourism building in town. All day he greeted travelers from around the globe with a firm handshake and a smile on his thin face. With long white hair down to his shoulders, he was tall and skinny and loved wearing cowboy boots and hats. He sported a thick handlebar mustache the same color as his hair.

Sid became a great friend while we rested in Beaver Creek, but he and Beat weren't the only friends we made. Usually, I'm extremely fearful of immigration officers. After crossing so many borders, especially with horses and being hassled at every single one, my relationship with these people who guard imaginary lines is not the best. The biggest scars I have with these people came when I was still a teen. After living in Canada for ten years legally, my family was asked to leave Canada. After growing up in one of the greatest countries in the world, when I got the news it was as if someone had pulled the ground from under me.

"They have given us thirty days to leave the country," my father said when he read the letter stating his work permit had been denied.

I cried. I screamed. I feared for the future. In my life plans, I never imagined going back to Brazil. Living in Canada since the age of nine, my best friends in the world lived five minutes from me. I couldn't write well in Portuguese. I was a defenseman on my hockey team. I had a horse named Amigo. Although my passport didn't say it, my heart was Canadian. Canada was my home.

In a desperate move, my father hired a lawyer who recommended that he apply from within Canada before those thirty days were up, stating humanitarian reasons. He did. We gathered letters from people in our community like priests, politicians, and businessmen. All of the years my father paid taxes. All of my volunteer work. Hundreds of photos and documents. Our file was so huge, it looked like a twenty-year-old murder case. After two years, the application was denied, and once again we were given thirty days to leave the country.

At a meeting with an immigration officer, we were placed behind a plexiglass wall, and treated as if we were criminals. I lost it. I yelled as my tears choked me, "We haven't done anything wrong! Why must you treat us like this?"

The woman on the other side of the glass, without batting an eye, looked at me and said, "Are you done, sir? Can I finish?" It was as if that plexiglass had her in another world.

I learned that the Canadian Immigration system is not as perfect as I had once imagined. They work on a points system where compassion and love don't fit in. I also learned my father shouldn't have moved us all to Canada with only a work permit. He renewed it for several years, but in the end, there was a maximum number of times he could do so. The lawyer who advised him to apply for humanitarian reasons from within Canada was a thief who took a lot of our money knowing it would never work. At that time, the rule was to apply from outside the country.

In the end, there was no one to blame. My parents did their best. The Canadian Immigration system was doing its best. The lawyer was making a living. But unfortunately, I was left heartbroken and completely at a loss.

After finishing my first year of journalism at Ryerson University, at the age of nineteen, I would have to return to my "home," a country I hadn't lived in since age nine and had last visited four years previously. I felt defeated, as if the entire world were against me. I felt as if I had been working on a painting for years called my future, and then one day without any warning, someone just walked up and painted over everything, every little detail, obliterating it with white paint. This was by far the worst moment of my life up to that point. But it was also a huge opportunity for me to learn that life is not a Disney movie. Life is really hard and sad and complicated. We all have problems and limitations.

However, thanks to free will, how you react to those difficulties is entirely up to you. Just like when wild horses are cornered, you can choose flight or fight. I chose to fight! So, with these bitter lemons life handed me at that moment, I made lemonade! In the end, the heartless woman behind the plexiglass gave us three months to organize our lives before we had to leave. I worked construction, framing ten to twelve hours a day, and raised enough money to backpack through Central America. I was about to leave without knowing if or how I would ever return.

However, the weekend before getting on a flight to Havana, Cuba, my life changed forever. I played my African bongo called a djembe (which in Mali means "everyone gather together or bringing people together") at my friend Shelagh's annual summer camp-out. Her mother, Sarah Crandall Haney, heard the drumming and came to chat with me. In her late fifties, she wore a brown poncho, and had dark hair down to her shoulders. On her wrists were the most beautiful boho-style turquoise bracelets I had ever seen.

"I love the sound of that instrument," she said with a smile that lit up the night. "What's it called?"

Sarah was the biggest Ian Tyson fan I had ever met and shared my passion for horses. We ended up talking until three in the morning. I told her about my desire to tell stories and try to build a more just world through journalism. She told me about her extraordinary work trying to save our oceans and her love for whales. A fluke hung on her necklace.

"Okay, kid, here's a book you need to read." Sarah passed me a copy of *Sea Shepherd: My Fight for Whales and Seals* written by Paul Watson, founder of the Sea Shepherd Conservation Society. "Now go back to the party," she added. "I need to sleep."

I didn't think much of our chat other than I loved this eccentric and kind woman and hoped I could be like her one day. Sarah was married to one of the inventors of Trivial Pursuit, Chris Haney. She helped create and develop an idea that gave life to one of the most successful board games of all time! As of 2014, Trivial Pursuit had sold 100 million games in twenty-six countries and seventeen languages. Instead of taking the money she earned and spending it on herself like many would, Sarah started helping different non-governmental organizations (NGOs), as well as people around the globe. The registered nurse is the co-founder of the Canadian Whale Institute and supports Salmon Coast Field Station in its efforts to save the wild Pacific salmon on Canada's west coast. She sat on the board of Save the Chimps, and with her three sisters, owned and operated Mount Wolfe Farm – a Community Supported Agriculture (CSA).

Thanks to that djembe, that humid summer night in Caledon, Ontario, my friend Shelagh, God, the Universe, and the alignment of the stars, this angel decided to help me as well. Sarah changed my life.

The following morning, she told her daughter Shelagh about our five-hour chat. My friend told her I was returning to Brazil and didn't know how I would be able to return to Canada to finish university. She told her mom the entire ordeal of how we had applied to stay in Canada and were refused. That's when Sarah intervened.

A week later, I cried like a baby around a lunch table with my parents at Mary Maw's house, my best friend Mark's mom. Sarah announced she would bring me back to Canada with a study permit and pay the astronomical price the university charged international students.

The pride my father had instilled in me was too strong to understand her kindness. "Sarah, I can't accept this."

"Filipe, yes, you can and you will," she said with her strong and loving motherly tone. I couldn't wrap my head around this woman spending so much money on my education. I wasn't her son. We had no blood relation. Hell, we had only met and spoken for the first time a week ago.

"I am not giving you this money. I am investing it in a brilliant young man who I'm sure will do great things with his education," she said, making me cry even more.

"Okay, but I will pay you back," I said to her, wiping the tears away.

"Filipe, I have been very fortunate to make a lot of money in my lifetime. You don't have to pay me back. This is an investment I am making in you." Her many bracelets clanked as she flipped her curly hair away from her face. "Your work as a journalist will be my payment."

"Fine, then when I can, I will do the same for another person who needs help to go to university," I replied.

"Deal, kid." She offered me her right hand, and we shook on it.

After that, I backpacked through Cuba, Guatemala, Honduras, Nicaragua, Costa Rica, and Panama. I wrote blogs about NGOs, poverty, desert beaches, and living in Rio de Janeiro for six months. I returned to Canada with my study permit to complete my studies. With my family's recent immigration history, it was a bureaucratic mess to obtain the visa, and I only got it because Ryerson's chair of Journalism, the talented Paul Knox, actually picked up the phone and called the Canadian Consulate in São Paulo and asked the consul at the time what the problem was with my application.

When I arrived back that first time, and every single time I have landed in Canada since, I got sent to the "other" immigration office to be questioned.

"What did you do in Canada?" is the question I always get when they scan my passport, just as the immigration officer in Beaver Creek had done days earlier. The difference was, this time, I actually got to know the human under the navy-blue uniform. He ended up being an amazing guy who I had the pleasure of sharing cold beer with. I never imagined that would happen in my entire life!

"You are the coolest immigration officer I have ever met," I said before cheering my new friend with the Yukon Golds he brought. He had spiky hair, a mustache, and reminded me a lot of my friend Mark Maw. We spent hours talking about what it was like working at this remote border crossing in the Yukon, my ride, and his future plan to return to Ontario where his girlfriend lived. Before we left Beaver Creek, with Mac and Smokey's shoes wearing out quickly, my new friend even helped me buy new shoes. One of his workmates was in Whitehorse buying groceries and offered to buy new shoes for my horses. With no tack or feed stores for the next 500 kilometers, these shoes would save our lives and my horses' feet.

"Thanks for coming by to chat," I said to him before we bid each other farewell.

ON A HOT WEDNESDAY MORNING, we began our ride towards Burwash Landing. After saying goodbye to all of our new friends, I kicked Mac up and Smokey followed close behind. That first morning, Smokey announced it was shark week, first biting Clara's back when she went to place his food under him and later my back while I inspected fresh bear scat.

"Smokey, there are enough things trying to eat me out here to have to worry about your sharp teeth, too," I said, giving him a hard look. His eyes showed the fire and chaos that inhabited his soul.

On our second day out, we rode by another RV park. While we let the horses graze in front of the place, Clara asked a nice elderly woman who worked there if we could spend the night with the horses, paying for our spot obviously.

"No horses allowed here," she said with a warm smile. We felt defeated. After we told her about what we were doing and where we were going, she let us know that just three kilometers down the road lived an outfitter who had more than sixty horses.

"I'm sure he would love to host you for a night. He has corrals, hay, and water," she told us before we bid her farewell. We felt hopeful. After a month of high-lining the horses and putting them in our small corral on the side of the Alaska Highway nearly every night due to the lack of ranches and farms, this place sounded like it was too good to be true.

"A real ranch with horses...here?" I asked Clara, not believing the news. I climbed on Smokey and ponied Mac south toward what sounded like heaven. When we arrived at the driveway for the ranch, I tied the horses to two trees and walked in. These were the directions the woman gave me.

"Hello, my name is Filipe. I'm riding two horses from Fairbanks to Calgary and was wondering if I can rest here tonight," I told a young man wearing an old red baseball cap.

"Let me go ask my dad," he said before running off to get his old man. Up in the north, I'd had little opportunity to ask for help. There were never any houses or ranches anywhere. Finally, here I was with my horses asking for a place to sleep. I'd done it a million times before on my earlier Long Rides, but it felt almost foreign after so many kilometers of solitude. Unlike my other journeys, where I never received a no and was always welcomed like family, this time it was different.

"I can't have your horses mixing with mine. I also don't want them calling out to each other. You can high line them next to my landing strip, 500 meters from here."

The outfitter's words seemed to have no meaning. I fought to understand what he was telling me, but it didn't make sense. As I looked around, I could see corrals and hay and water and horses. I couldn't believe it.

"Okay, thank you, sir. I saw you have a farrier here shoeing your horses. Do you mind if he shoes mine tonight?" I said before walking away.

"As long as you pay for it," he shot back.

"Yes, sir, of course, I will pay for it," I responded.

It was all too weird, a horseman being so cold, not asking what we needed, where we had come from, what we had seen. Instead, he shooed us away. On the other hand, it was better than nothing and, most importantly, Mac and Smokey would get new shoes. Plus, they would get shod by a professional farrier. I felt lucky!

I went back to the horses and Clara, and we made our way far enough down the runway to avoid bothering the outfitter. We found two good trees to tie up the horses and parked the motorhome near where we could keep an eye on them.

The farrier came shortly after and he was a character fit for an Agatha Christie novel. In his early thirties, a little overweight and with a wicked sense of humor, Patrick moved to Canada from Ireland a few years previously. "I ride broncs, cowboy at different ranches, and shoe horses," the redhead said before taking a swig of our Pendleton whiskey, part of his payment.

Mac and Smokey, who had been shod for the first time in their lives a few weeks before the journey, put up a fight. In the end, the Irish farrier and I were sweaty, exhausted, and drunk. His stories were epic, but my favorite was the one where he ended up shooting a guy in the leg, tying him to his packhorse, and bringing him down a mountain.

"We were taking care of cattle above the tree line one summer, and this guy went batshit crazy. Our camps were a day's ride away and we would see each other about once every few weeks. One day, he stopped answering me over the radio, so I went to check on him. When I arrived, he came out of the cabin with a knife saying he was going to kill me, so I pulled out my .22 revolver and shot him twice in the right leg," Patrick recalled while Clara and I listened intently.

The outfitter never came to say hello or ask a single question about our journey. The next morning, in a thick rain, I saddled the boys and rode out. I tied them up to the same trees I had the day prior and made my way to the ranch to thank him and the Irishman.

"It's raining," the outfitter said as he munched on a plate of bacon and eggs. "Why don't you rest another day and join us for breakfast?"

The smell literally made me drool. "Thank you, sir, but we have to ride on. Thanks for your help."

"I didn't do nothing," he answered.

"We do what we can," I shot back before thanking him and Patrick again and walking out. I stepped up onto the wet saddle and immediately regretted my words. With the rain making my life hell, I rode south dreaming of bacon and eggs.

As I passed another gate to his ranch, a few meters down the road, I noticed his truck was there, and he was sitting inside with the cab facing the road. I think he wanted to see the horses. I was learning that the north is a cold place, both literally and figuratively.

AFTER SIX LONG days on the road, we finally arrived in Burwash Landing, a small community in the middle of the Yukon wilderness. It was a hard ride that took us through no man's land. The weather had alternated from rain to sunshine at the drop of a hat. Clara saw one grizzly during the ride, but it ran off before the horses and I arrived.

"He was a pretty big one...ran across the road and up that hill," she told me over lunch.

We arrived in the small town of seventy-two residents Sunday afternoon. The local museum was still open, and Clara went to ask if there were any horse people in town. She received a no, so we found a small dirt road and camped for the night. The following morning, Clara drove to the local gas station and restaurant to buy a coffee for us and to fill up the motorhome with water and gasoline. While she chatted with the clerk about what we were doing, our luck changed.

Anita Dansereau, a blond, curly-haired woman was electric. "Oh, my! My best friend has horses, and she has a corral just eight kilometers from here! Let me call her."

By the time Clara arrived back to where we were camped, with coffees in hand, we had a place to rest our ponies.

"I met this amazing woman who has a friend with a corral halfway to Destruction Bay," Clara said, proud of her find. I could hardly believe it. A real corral. What a treat! The last time Mac and Smokey rested in a real corral, with lots of space to run, buck, and roll, was back in Tok, Alaska, more than 340 kilometers north.

The happiness I felt at that moment was better than winning an all-inclusive trip to Cancun. I promised my boys we would rest once we arrived in Burwash Landing. I felt bad to saddle them, so I decided to walk the eight kilometers (which turned out to be twelve) so they could both travel bareback and carry no weight.

Louisette Boudreau from Montreal and her husband Luke Johnson, a member of the Kluane First Nation, hosted our horses for three days at their stunning ranch. Luke had long, silky black hair that went down to the middle of his back, and a goatee on his long face. An avid trapper and horseman, he showed me his many pelts, from massive grizzlies to tiny gophers, and explained some of his people's hunting techniques.

"Sometimes we have to set up 100 snares to catch a single wolf," Luke said during a tour of his tanning shed. He told me about how his father loved horses and passed this passion down to him.

"Thank you for hosting the ponies and us at your ranch," I said to Luke during a party that never seemed to end. It was June 21, the longest day of the year. We were in a very special place, a land where the sun never sets in the summer! The summer solstice party started with us helping Louisette with the renovation of a trailer she was working on.

The French Canadian was a master carpenter. A black sun was tattooed on her flat stomach, around her belly button, and she worked in her bikini in the summer. "Hey, this is the Yukon. You have to enjoy the few nice days of the year," she said before letting out a strong laugh.

We drank cold beer and got to know the local Burwash Landing crowd. The interesting part was that although there were some people there who were born in the Yukon, many were from other provinces or even countries.

"We were on a bike tour of the Yukon last year and fell in love with the territory. This year we applied for a working-holiday visa and returned to work," a Spanish woman in her mid-thirties told me while her friend from France nodded along. Both were working at the local convenience store and restaurant on the reservation.

The afternoon after Luke and Louisette's summer solstice party, we continued south. The natural beauty of this stretch of the Yukon made me feel as if I were riding through an endless postcard: dramatic mountains, wide snaking turquoise rivers, and tilted trees known as a drunken forest crawling with various animal species. Glacier-fed lakes made this stretch one of the most beautiful I covered in all the Americas. We rode by intricate and colorful flowers like Draba, goldenweed, and Yukon lupin that only grew in the Yukon. They danced in the wind as small birds like the Yellow-rumped warbler, Dark-eyed junco and Say's phoebes kept nature's soundtrack sweet with their singing.

One day, a rusty blackbird, whose song sounds like a squeaky hinge, followed the horses and me for several kilometers. The sleek iridescent black bird would walk next to or behind the horses for a few meters, hopping on the tall grass, and then fly ahead of us. He kept doing this for about half an hour before he disappeared. I figured he was hoping the horses would drop a load full of seeds and delicious nutrients for him to eat. I loved his company!

My favorite Yukon bird, and one that became a common companion on this desolate stretch south, was the mighty raven. I learned an abundance about these large, matte-black birds that over the centuries have been the subject of mythology, folklore, art, and literature. The locals told me that in the north, for the indigenous cultures, the raven has been revered as a spiritual figure or godlike creature. What impressed me most about this mysterious bird were two things. The first is that to cool their bodies down, they stood on the side of the Alaska Highway, as still as statues with their beaks open wide. It was a weird scene I didn't get tired of seeing. The other interesting thing about the raven is its intelligence. The raven's brain is among the largest of any bird species and it is able to emulate sounds it hears! I thought that was so cool.

"Filipe, Filipe, Filipe," I would say to the birds as I rode by them with their open beaks. They never said my name back. I guess they're not parrots.

The most spectacular view during this stretch of the Yukon came during my ride around Kluane Lake. Flanked by Canada's tallest mountains, the sparkling blue lake is home to its largest ice field and Canada's highest peak (the 5,959-meter Mount Logan). Up before the sun rose, I was able to enjoy a phenomenon I have learned to enjoy thoroughly throughout my Long Rides. When you are in the mountains, the first light of day, when the sun peeks over the jagged rocks all around, the world turns pink for five to ten minutes. It's such a stunning tone, it makes everything look more beautiful!

After this quick period, something weird happens. It's as if the world goes into black and white for a while until the light returns and the day unfolds. To be able to take in this phenomenon while staring at Canada's tallest mountain was simply unbelievable, a true blessing. I quietly sat atop Mac, the saddle creaking once in a while, taking in the sunrise. I wanted this view to burn itself onto my soul, like a brand is burned on a cow's hide, so I could take it with me forever. Although this area stunningly displays the Yukon's supreme and untouched natural beauty, it also serves as a perfect example of how climate change is affecting the north faster than other places.

"The lake has dropped about two meters in the past couple of years," Luke told me before we left his house in Burwash Landing. For more than 300 years, the Slims River carried the glacial runoff that fed Kluane Lake. Since the spring of 2016, the Kaskawulsh glacier has receded so much that its runoff no longer makes it to the Slims River. Instead, it began flowing down a new river.

"This has affected the people and animals that live here," Luke told me. "We can't fish in traditional spots anymore. Spawning areas for whitefish are now above the water, and the Slims River Valley has become a desert with winds blowing sand across the highway."

With my head tilted down, I felt that sand hit me in the face for the hour it took me to cross the valley on horseback. It was apocalyptic. The lake, which had receded a full kilometer to leave islands standing completely out of the water, was otherworldly and sad.

11

THE ROAD TO WHITEHORSE

The day after crossing Kluane Lake, during a foggy morning in the middle of nowhere, a young man in his early twenties stopped me. He was riding his bicycle from Chicago to Alaska. He was a fair-skinned man with curly hair poking out from under his bike helmet. "Are you the Brazilian who is traveling on horseback?"

A bit surprised at the question, I answered, "Yes, I am. Why?"

"Okay, beyond Haines Junction, there is an RV park and campground called Otter Falls. The manager heard about your trip and wants you to stay there," he said before pedaling off.

I thanked my curly-haired messenger before he disappeared into the fog behind me. A few kilometers down the road, I ran into another visitor. This one was not as friendly.

"Hey!" I yelled at the top of my lungs. Mac and Smokey shifted their ears back and forth, alarmed by my voice and my shaking knees. Just in front of us, on the opposite side of the highway, sat a gut-churning sight: a grazing grizzly bear!

This was the first time my horses and I encountered one of these petrifying animals. We were about seven meters from the skinny beast. When I spotted him, I stopped the horses. First, I saw his fluffy ears, then the protruding hump on his shoulders, and finally his small, beady eyes. Its caramel fur stuck up in patches. He was an adolescent, not fully grown, but big enough to scare the soul out of my body. To say the least, he looked like he'd had a hard winter.

I'd read in a book about how to travel safely through bear country weeks before. I'd been informed that grizzly bears can run at fifty-five kilometers per hour, climb trees, and swim. Now, these words plagued my thoughts.

"Hey, bear! Hey, bear!" I yelled again, trying to get him to see us.

Finally, the grizzly lazily raised his head and studied us for a few seconds. Unamused, he dropped his long muzzle back to the patch of bright yellow dandelions.

My mustangs, who had tried to run off a million times at the sight of anything that looked remotely like a bear since we began the journey, simply watched the creature, waiting for direction. Unsure of what to do next, I trusted my gut and rode on. Just five meters from the beast, I held my breath, waiting for my horses to blow up at any second. Or worse, excite the bear.

Nothing happened. He kept eating and my boys kept walking. I couldn't get over how skinny and sickly the bear looked. He almost ate in slow motion. His skin sagged from his big bones. He didn't look anything like the obese bears on the Discovery Channel.

This was just one of two bears we encountered that week near Haines Junction. The second, startled by the sound of the horseshoes hitting gravel, stuck his head out from behind a spruce tree. He stood on his hind legs and stared at us with curiosity. As soon as I made eye contact with the big brown bear, he took off into the woods. I'm not sure who looked more scared, the cowboy or the bear. His reaction when he saw me and the way he stood behind the tree was so human. It was as if there were a person inside a bear costume.

Clara, driving our trusty thirty-year-old support vehicle, spotted two more grizzlies ahead of me. "One was a big one, but I honked the horn and he ran off."

On that hot afternoon, we enjoyed a gift from a friendly stranger: canned moose meat (a first for me). With the amount of bear scat and tracks that I saw every day, I was extremely lucky not to have run into more bears in that region. However, it wasn't just the bears that gave me trouble during this long, wild stretch of nothing.

On a chilly morning, while I trekked the Alaska Highway, a swamp lining the ditch on both sides, three loud BMW motorcycles startled us. Because of the strong headwind blowing that day, we didn't hear the engines' roar until they were passing us. When the first motorcycle screamed by at 100 kilometers per hour, my mustangs took flight. I was riding Smokey. Mac galloped past me, his lead rope dragging on the ground. The other two motorcycles struggled to overtake us.

As my cowboy hat flew off, I remember thinking, *Wow, we must be going fast*. I fought to stop Smokey, pulling back on the reins hard, but he just kept running like we were on the final stretch of the Kentucky Derby. When I saw an opening on the left side of the road, I turned Smokey toward it and eventually ran him into some small trees. Mac followed behind. It took me an entire kilometer to finally stop my out-of-control mustangs.

The irony is that when the last bike finally overtook us, a small, tattered Brazilian flag flapped in the wind. When the horses were tied up, and my hands finally stopped shaking, Clara and I laughed at the thought that some crazy Brazilians on motorcycles nearly killed us.

But the biggest villains in the Yukon were not the bears or the motorcycles. The mosquitoes are truly larger than life. "I just hit this thing five times and it won't die," I yelled to Clara while we let the horses graze on the side of the road one night.

The mosquitoes were so bad at times the only way to ride was with fly masks and a gallon of bug spray. The horses and I looked ridiculous, all three with our faces covered by a light mesh and reeking of citronella. Big Mac became Mad Max! But with the flies, horseflies, and mosquitoes trying to enter every cavity on your face all day long, vanity didn't matter. Their buzzing was a constant soundtrack from the moment we opened our eyes to the second we fell asleep.

I was in the middle of the Yukon, and instead of cars, there was the sound of millions, trillions of quadrillions of blood-thirsty mosquitoes. I was astounded by how loud they were. It was as if I were in downtown Toronto, listening to the constant buzzing of cars traveling down the Gardiner Expressway.

The bugs nearly drove me crazy, and they may have pushed Clara all the way insane. One night while I fed the horses after a long day, I watched her open a box of pasta and throw the entire contents in the garbage.

"Why did you do that?" I asked.

"Oh, my God, I have no idea! I was supposed to throw the pasta into the pan and the box in the garbage," she said, staring at the brand-new pasta, now in the dirty garbage, the blue pasta box still in her hand. The Yukon was getting to us.

At four kilometers per hour and thirty kilometers a day, four days after leaving Burwash Landing, we arrived at Haines Junction. Louisette had a friend in town with an empty corral behind her home who was kind enough to host the horses and us for two days.

"I'm not in town, but you can put your horses in the corral and park your motorhome next to it," she said over the phone before we arrived. That's what we did. She hadn't had a horse in the corral in months so the grass was tall, up to the horses' bellies. Mac and Smokey marveled at the bright green grass and immediately dropped their heads and started mowing it down.

"You boys deserve this," I said before filling their water trough. In Haines Junction, we visited the local visitor's center. It told the story of the First Nations people who lived in that area for hundreds of years. I tried to speak to them for an interview, but unfortunately, I was told I had to book an appointment weeks in advance. Instead, we focused on taking care of Mac and Smokey, washed our clothes, and ate real food. It was a nice treat before making our final push for Whitehorse.

It was hard to believe we had already ridden so far. When we left Fairbanks, Whitehorse looked so far away on the map, so many days of riding and so many obstacles along the way. Yet now we were only 154 kilometers away from the Yukon's capital.

After two days' rest, I saddled the ponies and rode out of Haines Junction with a stunning view of the jagged mountains behind me. That day, I saw three porcupines on the side of the road. Thirty thousand long, sharp quills cover a porcupine's body. Their sharp nails are perfect for climbing trees. Their appearance, combined with their slow and chunky demeanor, make them look prehistoric. I saw several porcupines during my ride through the Yukon.

Our next milestone on the journey south was Otter Falls Campground. "Oh, boy, how I have been waiting to meet you!" Wally Bootsma said as we shook hands.

"I know! Your messenger told me a few weeks ago," I responded, telling him about my encounter with the curly-haired cyclist.

Wally was a character. He looked like Richard Simmons. Curly hair in an Afro, light skin, and a huge zest for life. "Let's go for a ride in my golf cart. I'm going to take you two somewhere cool. Hold on!" We zoomed off at what seemed like a million miles an hour.

After a short ride, we stopped to take in a gorgeous view of two large mountains and a sea of trees. Wally handed me a driver and a can filled with multicolored golf balls. "Let's play a game and see who can hit it the farthest."

We spent half an hour smiling like kids, whaling golf balls, and yelling, "Fore!"

The following morning, before we left, Wally graciously donated two bags of non-perishable food for our ride. "Be safe out there, you two. Feel free to call if you need anything," he said.

I thanked our new friend and continued south.

That afternoon, we visited the Long Ago People's Place in Champagne. A re-creation of a First Nations village, it had traditional living structures as well as tools and hunting re-creations. Walking inside the village, I felt as if I had traveled back in time.

"It is important for me to share my culture with the people of the world," said Harold Johnson, the museum's founder and our tour guide. He'd built the place with his own hands. A soft-spoken man, he wore a blue and black bandana tied on his head with his long, gray hair flowing out the back.

We got to see a traditional cache, where First Nations people would store food they'd harvested during the summer for the long winters, usually built up high so animals couldn't get to it easily. We saw a smokehouse where fish and meat were smoked and even learned about the importance of eating gophers.

"My people relied on eating gopher meat because these animals live off different weeds, flowers, and grasses that offer vitamins and nutrients," Harold explained as we toured the village. While he told his stories, he rolled a small and tight tobacco cigarette.

The tour ended with warm bannock, a fried flatbread, and tea. Clara and I loved the Long Ago People's Place and Harold. He was an amazing host and guide.

From Champagne, we battled a terrible heatwave as we inched closer and closer to Whitehorse. We had trekked into the heart of summer. For Canada Day, we drank cold Canadians with a friendly German who lived in a cabin in the middle of nowhere. He was an intense man who'd fought with the Special Forces for years.

"I think it's so cool what you are doing," he said as we toasted Canadians on his front lawn. He took big puffs of a thick joint rolled with tobacco and marijuana.

The following day, we met a French expat who allowed us to turn our horses out in a corral behind his log home. "I came here because there are too many people in Europe. There are tough times coming with all of the immigrants showing up," he told us in a thick French accent. Like the German from the previous night, he also smoked joints non-stop. Unlike the German, he did not mix in tobacco.

A day or two later, while I walked next to the horses early one morning, I came upon a road crew working on the Alaska Highway. There were three men with shovels covering holes and one driving a big tractor. Two of the men, both Caucasian and in their early forties, had terrible looks on their faces as they shoveled tar into the holes.

The third man's smile was larger than life. "Good morning, beautiful horses!" he said with a thick West-African accent and lively enthusiasm.

I got such a strong feeling of how thankful this new immigrant was to be in Canada. To have a job. To have his health. To have an opportunity at a better life. His smile was so pure, his demeanor so humble. It was as if I could read his entire life story in his eyes, the portals to the soul. He felt blessed. I wondered where he was born. What kind of life did he have back home? How did he get to the Yukon? Some Canadians, like the two men who worked away in a terrible mood that morning, had no idea of how lucky they were to live in such an amazing country, a bubble in the midst of an unjust world. It's only when you've seen the dark that you are truly able to enjoy the light.

"Have a great day," I said to my new friend after telling him the horses' names.

"You, too, man, a beautiful day," he responded, working away.

In this section of land, although we didn't see any, we crossed signs of several herds of wild horses. Apparently, many years back, an outfitter, tired of the hunting industry, turned all of his horses loose next to the Alaska highway. The horses adapted to the wild, and today have formed several herds that can be seen next to the highway before you reach Whitehorse.

Worried that the studs would give us trouble, I tried to cross this area as quickly and quietly as possible. All day, I rode by horse manure and tracks. Smokey had other plans. The mustang, who was cut days prior to our journey's beginning, wanted to meet these wild horses so badly. One day, he puffed his chest out and began whinnying as loud as he could in the direction where their smell was coming from.

"Stop, Smokey! Stop!" I tried to shut him up, but he wasn't having any of it.

"Come out here if you're brave enough," Smokey yelled towards the forest with his head held high. Mac, his slower brother, looked around, confused. We rode south quickly, and I prayed that the studs would not come looking for a fight. Luckily, they weren't brave enough, and a day before arriving in Whitehorse, we rode into a beautiful property called Heart Bar Ranch.

"Filipe and Clara! We are happy to host you and your horses,"

Gail, the owner, said. As luck would have it, we arrived during the week Gail ran day camps for excited little girls from the area. It was too much cuteness to handle as little blonde girls ran around laughing and playing on their horses.

"We teach them how to do chores, basic riding, and some equestrian vaulting," Gail explained over a dinner of hot dogs and Caesar salad. Gail had a raspy voice and kind eyes. Her blonde hair, tied in two braids, and her light skin made her look like a Scandinavian queen. She was big and strong, but her heart was even bigger. She started organizing these clinics in 1997, and although the days are long and tiring, she believes she is helping create a better generation.

"I think horses lend an authenticity, a reality to a person's life that's hard to come by these days," she told me as she fidgeted with her coffee cup.

"So much of our life is made of entertainment, something to do to pass the time, instead of real stuff that has to happen, like caring for animals. If the work doesn't get done, somebody dies or suffers. It's something real in a world that has so much that isn't real."

I couldn't have agreed more with Gail. Watching the young girls feed the animals on the ranch made me think of my own upbringing and all the lessons horses taught me over the years. Hard work, focus, determination, leadership, patience, love. It was a long list. The truth is, if I hadn't grown up roping and rodeoing, I would have never finished these Long Rides. I would have quit when the going got tough. The horse has made me who I am today. The horse has made me a better human being.

Feeling inspired by my talk with Gail and the little girls working at the ranch, I sat on a bale of hay and drank *mates* with Clara while watching Smokey and Mac graze. It had been a long and hard road since leaving Fairbanks, nearly two months before. I was over the moon to be only thirty kilometers from our next resting point and a major hurdle on this Last Long Ride.

Finally, on Friday, July 5, fifty days after leaving Fairbanks, Alaska, I rode a gray horse and ponied a buckskin into Whitehorse. To say I felt proud of my two mustangs was an understatement. With their heads held high and muscles bulging, we arrived twelve days ahead of schedule. My ponies looked like they had walked fifty-one kilometers, not 951.

The Yukon is not for the faint of heart. It's for dreamers, like the men and women who traveled to this territory in search of riches during the Klondike Gold Rush. It's for those who work hard and don't quit. It's for brave cowboys and wild horses!

12

WHITEHORSE

In Whitehorse, we felt at home and were welcomed like family. "Filipe, it's so nice to be hosting you guys. I'm reading your book right now," Jocelyn Barrett said with a grin before passing me a cold Budweiser.

Reading my first book, *Long Ride Home*, she knew that I always drank Bud while crossing the United States. A lawyer, originally from Kuujjuaq, Quebec, she and her husband, John Van der Meer, lived in a gorgeous log home just north of Whitehorse with a chestnut mare and a bay gelding. John's father, Sid Van der Meer, whom we met in Beaver Creek, graciously secured this extraordinary layover for us.

"My dad hasn't stopped talking about you guys since you came through," said John while he flipped the elk sausages we would have for dinner that night.

As Jocelyn took us to meet her horses, she told us about her life growing up in the remote community of Kuujjuaq. The largest community in Nunavik, and a former Hudson's Bay Company outpost, had a total population of 2,754 people. No roads linked Kuujjuaq to even its closest neighbor. In fact, none of the fourteen villages in Nunavik were linked by roads. The only way to gain access was by snowmobile, dogsled, plane, or canoe.

"My parents moved to Kuujjuaq permanently in 1978 when Dad worked with what is now called Indigenous Relations and Northern Affairs Canada," she explained. In 1979, her father became one of the first employees of the Kativik Regional Government, which was established after the signing of the James Bay and Northern Quebec agreement between Quebec, Canada, the Inuit of Quebec, and the Cree of Quebec.

"Mom was a teacher for the Kativik School Board in Kuujjuaq for her whole career," said Jocelyn.

She told us how she loved living up there except for one small problem. "When I was a little girl, I loved horses so much, but there was no way to have a horse up there. We don't even have a word for horses in my native tongue." The petite lawyer explained the word used for "horse," *qimmiqjuaq*, literally means "big dog" in Inuktitut, a language in which she was fluent.

Eventually, Jocelyn left the small remote community for another northern community — Whitehorse — where she finally got her big dog!

"It's kind of ironic how I left one remote northern community for another," she said, laughing, "but at least here I can have horses."

And thanks to her and John, my horses had a spacious pasture in which to fill their bellies and rest their hooves. We went about exploring the city of roughly 25,000 people — northern Canada's major urban hub.

"Please take our truck. It will be much easier for you to get around," John said, passing me the keys to his brand-new Dodge Ram. We tried to say no, but he and Jocelyn didn't give us a chance.

We arrived in time for the final day of the Adaka Cultural Festival, our first stop. In its ninth year, the festival, whose name means "coming into the light" in the Southern Tutchone language, cele-brates the arts and culture of the Yukon's fourteen First Nations. Since the United Nations declared 2019 the Year of Indigenous Languages, this event celebrated the eight First Nations' language groups in the Yukon in all aspects of the festival. I couldn't believe the coincidence after spending the previous night talking to Jocelyn about her speaking Inuktitut and the importance of not forgetting our roots.

Charlene Alexander, the executive director of the Yukon First Nations Culture and Tourism Association, observed, "There's a real sense of now or never when we discuss First Nations languages. They are in danger of extinction."

In nearly all of the communities in the Yukon, only the elders can still speak their language fluently due to the effects of residential schools. It was heartbreaking to hear stories about how First Nations children were shamed and mistreated for speaking their native tongues.

While he worked on a stunning buffalo carving, a First Nation artist from Teslin said, "I know the weight of the Bible, literally. The missionaries used to make me hold Bibles with my arms spread out. If I lowered my hands below my shoulders, they would add another one on top."

Despite the hard stories I heard, there was a real sense of hope in people's eyes and smiles. I learned about various initiatives being conducted to save these native languages, like the Tr'ondëk Hwëch'in government in Dawson City turning to social media for help. With weekly Facebook videos featuring Hän language words, they hoped to reach the younger generation. Other native governments had study groups and offered native languages in elementary and high schools throughout the territory.

While exploring the festival next to the Yukon River, we learned how to tan a moose hide and how to make a canoe using that hide. I couldn't get over how hard it was to tan a hide. My arms were limp after only a few minutes scraping the fat off the inside of the hide (what the Natives call fleshing). Harder than the work was not puking from the intense smell. It reeked like a decaying corpse, a stench I was not able to rid from my hands for days, no matter how many times I washed them.

After this process, we learned the hide must be soaked for six days, stretched on a frame, scraped again, smoked, soaked for another two days in a washing solution, stretched again, and then one must wring it lightly and stretch it on a frame for a final time. It's not an easy process, but one that has been extremely important for First Nations groups all over Canada for thousands of years. Moose-hide was and is used to this day to make clothing, drums, and canoes. I loved going to the festival and learning more about the First Nations' story in the Yukon.

WHILE RESTING IN WHITEHORSE, I decided to get my now shaggy and out-of-control hair a trim, something that proved to be more difficult than I ever imagined. First, I had to call eleven different salons before I found one that had time to book an appointment that week!

When the fifth salon told me they only had an open spot in two weeks. Clara announced, "After this trip, I'm going to learn how to cut hair and move to Whitehorse."

Nearly an hour on the phone later, I finally found a place that would do it that day. Slickers Hair Design by Gloria wasn't located in the downtown core nor was it a real salon. It was a small office located in Gloria's quaint yellow and white home. The strong smell of stew cooking in the next room permeated the house. I could hear the pressure pan whistling like a train.

"Filipino?" asked the brunette when I walked into her home.

"No, my name is Filipe," I replied to the hairdresser who was born in the Philippines.

"Yes, Filipino," she responded with a warm smile. This went on for a few minutes when I decided to accept my inevitable fate. In order to get my hair cut, I would have to become my new alias. I've been called worse things.

"Is okay I check my corn?" my hairdresser asked me exactly one minute into my cut.

"Um, yes, I guess," I said as she already made her way into the kitchen, scissors still in hand. After about three minutes, she returned chewing corn while she announced, "Almost."

Small pieces of corn hit me in the back of the head as I watched her through the spotted mirror in front of me. By this point, I was a little worried about what my haircut would look like. Since I was in the middle of the Yukon and wore a cowboy hat every day, I decided to relax and get to know this chef-hairdresser. Gloria told me she lived in Hong Kong for several years before immigrating to Canada.

"Very hard life there (Hong Kong)...(I) work like slave for little bit money," she explained before leaving to check on her corn once more.

According to Statistics Canada's census of 2016, the Filipino community in the Yukon comprises one of the largest language groups, with 805 people speaking Tagalog as a first language. Of the most visible minorities living in the Yukon, Filipinos comprise the biggest group at 39.7 percent. According to Gloria, it's the work opportunities that bring her people to the far North.

"The Yukon has many jobs for people who don't mind work hard," Gloria said.

Sporting a fresh mullet and reeking of corn, I received a very special visit. My childhood friend, Shelagh Haney, rented a van and drove out to the Yukon. The daughter of Sarah, the angel who changed my life, planned to stay at her family's cabin and to see us.

"I will see you in Whitehorse," she'd told me over coffee in Toronto several weeks prior to my journey's beginning. Shelagh is a woman of her word. Not only did she drive from Ontario to spend six days with us (a total of 5,370 kilometers), she also brought a special surprise.

"No way, you came!" I yelled when I saw my friend Terry Indellicato sneak out from the bar where we met Shelagh. I couldn't believe it. Terry and I have been friends since high school where we used to play soccer for the Robert F. Hall Wolfpack. After we graduated, we lived together through most of university. We both studied journalism at Ryerson, hosted our own radio show for years, and partied way too much.

"I missed you, baby," Terry said with a smile on his Italian face. After I got over the shock, we celebrated Terry and Shelagh's arrival before driving out to her family's remote cabin.

The cabin sat in the middle of nowhere, about half an hour outside of the picturesque town of Carcross. Surrounded by tall green grass and giant spruce trees, the quaint blue wooden cabin had a red door, fireplace, and a stunning view. As I stood out on the deck, I could see two dramatic mountains on both sides of the structure and forest all around. "Shelagh, this is heaven," I told her.

We toasted my friends' arrival with Yukon Golds. "Cheers!" we yelled before taking a sip of the cold beer we nicknamed Yookie Golds.

Together with Terry, Shelagh, and Clara, we rested like kings and queens for two days at the cabin, eating way too much and laughing until our faces hurt. We saw a black bear going to the bathroom (number 2). That answered the frequently asked question: Does a bear shit in the woods?

A big moose came by right next to the cabin, too. "Wow, he's so big!" Terry said as we watched the large animal graze.

The horses rested at a ranch just outside of Whitehorse owned by a friend of Shelagh's mom named Mary Walden. Along with her husband Blaine, they had a horse and more than a dozen huskies they used for mushing.

"You can't buy this kind of tranquility and peace," Mary told me while we ate the delicious moose meat and ricotta lasagna she'd prepared specially for us. It was the best lasagna I have ever eaten in my life! Hands down!

Mary, who used to work for CBC News, explained how she got tired of "feeding the news machine," and decided to move out here with Blaine. "The only worry I have these days is if there's a bear in the front yard or not," she said laughing.

Having Smokey and Mac rest at Mary's while we spent time at Shelagh's cabin was an amazing break for Clara and me not to have to wake up at 6:30 a.m. to feed our four-legged kids.

"I can't believe we slept in until 8 a.m.," I said to Clara on our first morning at the cabin. It felt so weird waking up so late and not hearing the bell fastened to Mac's neck in the middle of the night that made my heart jump as I fought to remember where I was.

After a lovely few days with my friends, I was sad having to say goodbye to Shelagh and Terry. "I'm going to miss you kids. Thank you so much for coming." I said.

I can't even begin to explain how seeing these old friends gave me the power to continue my Last Long Ride.

AFTER A WEEK RESTING and buying all the provisions we needed for the next 1,000 kilometers of nothing, it was time to ride out of White-horse. But first, we made our way to a ranch owned by Angelique Bjork, a friend of John and Jocelyn's, to get the ponies shod. I gave my motivational talk to a group of 4-H girls. It was an amazing opportunity to share my story to wide-eyed little horse girls. Afterward, I spent an hour answering their excited questions.

"Where are your horses from?"

"Do they like apples?"

"Can I ride your horses?"

"Can I give them apples?"

When it came time to ride out of the ranch, all of the young girls jumped on their horses and rode out with me. After so many days crossing the Yukon alone, it was an emotional scene. After a few minutes, the girls returned to the ranch, and Angelique continued south with me for another couple of kilometers.

"Please stay safe out there, especially with the recent murders down the highway," the barrel racer said before she returned to the ranch.

The murders Angelique referred to were of two tourists found shot dead next to the Alaska Highway near Liard Hot Springs. Another body was found later. The news rocked the north, and Clara and me especially because the young people killed were a transnational couple just like us. The young man was from Australia and the girl from the United States, both around our age.

"I can't believe we have to worry about being murdered in northern Canada being from Argentina and Brazil," Clara said while we read up on the story online. On CBC News, Jason Proctor reported, "Kam McLeod and Bryer Schmegelsky are believed to have killed Lucas Fowler (23) and Chynna Deese (24), before killing Leonard Dyck (64) within a six-day timeframe."

The news was not only extremely sad, but scary! We were worried. It wasn't just Angelique who warned us, either. Another gentleman told us not to sleep on the side of the road no matter what. Clara and I simply laughed at one another nervously. We only traveled thirty kilometers a day. The next town, Teslin, was 200 kilometers away. We would have to sleep on the side of the road every night until we arrived in the small town and would continue to do so after.

The gentleman was right to warn us. When Lucas Fowler and Chynna Deese were shot and killed by the teen killers, the victims were parked on the side of the road for several hours with their broken-down van. There was nothing we could do but ride on and hope for the best.

On our second day on the road, while Clara and I searched for a good place to eat lunch, we met an extraordinary character. An elderly fellow pulled up in his four-wheeler. "I used to have horses too, you know," Donald Bernier told me.

We chatted for a bit, and Don invited us to come to his house to check out the belt buckles he made from polished stones. "Come see my shop, and we can rest your horses on my front lawn," he said with a big smile.

Don's house, overlooking Marsh Lake, was gorgeous and had a beautifully trimmed lawn for the boys to feast on. Don wore a stained red trucker hat, a western shirt with overalls over top of linen pants. With every third word spoken, his tongue would push its way out of his mouth to wet his dry lips. Don was retired, a widower, and probably a little lonely. For an hour, he gave us a tour of his shop and showed us how he made the stone belt buckles.

"I don't sell these, I just give them as presents," he said while he polished a pink Rubellite. At the end, he showed us his stunning home overlooking a large lake and offered me a drink of whisky and Sprite. We chatted about his life working as a guide in the Yukon and for a large telecommunications company, his love for the north, and the recent passing of his wife.

Don fell in love with Clarita. "Here, I want you to have these." He gave Clara a belt buckle and two stones before we said goodbye.

After bidding our new friend farewell, we continued south. We saw several bears a day and tried to stay sane despite the trillion mosquitoes hovering over our bodies constantly. We also woke up to every strange noise at night wondering if we would be brutally murdered by the teen killers. They never showed up, thankfully, but another unwelcome guest did.

A few days before arriving in Teslin, 178 kilometers south of Whitehorse, we were awakened by the horses trying to run off from the high line.

"What was that?" Clara cried out from beneath the covers.

"I'm not sure. The horses are scared of something." I shone my headlamp at my frightened ponies. The darkness was eerie after so many long nights of sunlight. Now, in mid-July, the sun was finally setting again.

Everything went still. Quiet. The only sound was my heart pounding inside my chest. The horses, wide-eyed and with their ears pitched forward, looked off into the dark forest, periodically blowing air out of their nostrils.

All of a sudden, the silence was broken by twigs breaking. A few seconds passed before more cracked, making Mac and Smokey want to run off again. Luckily, the high line stayed fastened to the two willows I'd tied it to, and the horses got turned around.

"There's something walking around out there. I think it's a moose," I told Clara. Her eyes went wider than those of the ponies.

I lied. I knew it was a bear. When I shone the light where the horses were looking, I saw its glowing red eyes. The snapping twigs also gave him away. It sounded like a human walking, trying to sneak around in the forest.

Outside, holding my headlamp with my left hand and four wisps of hay with my right, I yelled, "Get out of here!" If the bear came for me, I decided I would throw the hay in his face. Not sure if it would help, but it's all I had. Maybe he was allergic. I yelled for a few minutes while Clara slammed on the horn of the old motorhome.

"You guys are okay," I said to Mac and Smokey before giving each two flakes of hay. "Everyone just relax."

I tried to sound way more confident than I felt. Truth is, I was shitting my pants! I tied the bell on Mac's neck, something I had forgotten to do for the first time in months. Luckily, the bear disappeared into the night, and we went back to sleep, or tried to, anyway.

The following day, while I rode in the early morning, I received a welcome guest! A stunning Sara Orangetip butterfly landed on the horn of my saddle. Measuring about three centimeters in wingspan, it was a pale yellow with bright red-orange wingtips. At that moment, as I sat in awe watching the stunning butterfly move to the rhythm of my saddle, I was reminded of something I had once read. Some believe dead loved ones return in spirit, revisiting the living as butterflies, physical representations of the human soul. The image of my great-aunt, America Lobo, came to me. The sweetest lady in the world, she helped raise me along with my grandmother.

My great-aunt had passed away a few weeks previously, the day Clara and I flew to Canada to begin my Last Long Ride. She loved me and supported my rides from day one. She even kept a photo of me with Frenchie, Bruiser, Dude (the horses I rode from Canada to Brazil) with her at all times to show people she met. After a minute or two, the butterfly opened its beautiful and intricate wings and flew away like a flower in the wind.

"*Tchau tia, te amo,*" I said. Goodbye, aunt, I love you.

BEFORE ARRIVING IN TESLIN, we received a visit from our Albertan parents! Marie and Rocky Aitken, who lent us our motorhome, rode their motorcycle 2000 kilometers north to see us.

"How was the trip?" I asked Marie after we shared a hug.

"It was great! We are so excited to see you two," Marie's bright smile and braids made her look like a teen.

We found a place to tie the horses and shared a warm cup of coffee next to the Alaska Highway. While we enjoyed our drinks, Marie told me about how she met a Kentucky man traveling on his motorcycle towards Alaska.

"We met at the hotel last night, and when I told him why we were traveling, he couldn't believe the coincidence. "He told us, 'I just finished reading his book!'"

Marie retold the story with excitement and before we even finished our cups of coffee, the Kentucky man arrived with his brother-in-law. We spent a few minutes chatting, and after taking a photo together, they took off, headed for Alaska.

For the next few days, Rocky and Marie made regular visits bearing many gifts from giant cookies to warm soup and cold beer. It was like having my mom and dad with us for a few days and I loved it. Their guidance and love made me feel at home in the middle of the Yukon. But having a mom and dad around also meant I had to hear a lot of "We are worried about you."

"Filipe, this bridge is dangerous. Why don't you trailer the horses across?" Rocky asked while we discussed a colossal bridge ahead. I would have to cross it to leave Teslin, my next major hurdle.

"I think it's the only way," Marie chimed in. I explained to Rocky and Marie, who were right to be worried, that I was in the middle of an adventure. This was my day-to-day. I loved the adrenaline, and I'd planned for these moments. Being cautious and as safe as possible, I, too, was worried about the bridge.

I was taking a calculated risk. At 584 meters, the Nisutlin Bay Bridge is the longest bridge on the Alaska Highway, and it has a metal mesh deck. Since driving over its metal mesh months earlier on our drive up to Alaska, I feared riding over this monster with my horses. Fact was, I feared not even being able to get them to step onto the bridge! It looked like a scarier version of a cattle guard. However, like many times before on these journeys, I decided to worry about the bridge when I came to it.

The day before arriving in Teslin, the Gods of Adventure decided to host a meeting of wanderers next to the Alaska Highway. It all started when a tall, skinny German who was cycling down to Ushuaia stopped to chat with us. With a bright smile, he pulled up next to the horses. "I heard about you from another biker who passed me going north a month ago," he said.

We spent about ten minutes chatting and sharing stories from the road when another adventurer, using a different mode of transportation, pulled over. His name was Ivan Lobo, and he was riding a heavy BMW motorcycle which looked as if it had been ridden hard. "Are you the crazy Brazilian horseman?" the bearded man asked in Portuguese after pushing the visor on his helmet up.

With both of us so far from home, we shared a strong hug only two souls who come from the same country can share. Ivan had heard about me at a rest stop a few kilometers north and was excited to meet me and the legendary horses I rode. "We are crazy, my friend! We make the world turn," he said while hugging Mac's thick neck.

Ivan had already ridden from Brazil to Alaska and was now heading down to the Nevada desert for the Burning Man festival. A Brazilian traveling on horseback, a German with a yellow bicycle, and another Brazilian on a heavy motorcycle. It sounded like the beginning of a good joke. We spent an hour laughing and sharing stories on the side of the Alaska Highway.

Cars drove by slowly, drivers peering, confused as to what the hell was happening at that moment. Magic! That's what. Three men who for some reason were meant to meet right then and there. All three, thousands of kilometers from home in the middle of the Yukon, all wandering, none lost. It's a moment I will never forget.

After saying goodbye to my new friends, I continued south. What I didn't know was that Ivan would proceed to the Teslin restaurant, gas station, and motel and tell everyone there about my story.

"Are you the Brazilian horseman who has crossed the Americas?" a Mexican couple in a colorful Volkswagen hippie van asked an hour later. They pulled over when I answered yes. In a few minutes, more travelers joined: a Brazilian couple riding up to Alaska on a single motorcycle; an elderly Brazilian on another BMW motorcycle; and another Mexican couple.

"You are a legend in Teslin, thanks to Ivan," the Mexican motorcyclist said while we all laughed. On the side of the highway, we all contemplated the reasons we chose to live great adventures.

"It doesn't cost anything to dream. It's free. Anyone can do it," the elderly Brazilian motorcyclist said. He had already ridden his motorcycle through nearly all the countries in the Americas.

We all agreed. Our dreams had brought us here. But the important thing is that all of us had the courage to turn them into a reality, to take the first step. The rest, as all of us knew well by now, the Universe took care of!

13

TESLIN

"Welcome to your home for the next few days," Lisa Dewhurst said before giving me a hug. Our host in Whitehorse, Jocelyn Barrett, put us in touch with her friend Lisa weeks before we were to arrive in Teslin. They both had horses and thanks to these majestic animals, had become good friends.

Already with a cold beer in hand while I got to know everyone, I thanked Lisa for hosting us. Mac and Smokey enjoyed their rest on the shores of Teslin Lake while we heard stories from Lisa's husband, Darcy, an avid hunter and trapper from the Teslin First Nation.

Over a delicious meal of moose ribs, mashed potatoes, and salad, Darcy told us, "After you harvest your moose, you place your gun in the bottom of the fridge, then you put the meat on top. You only get your gun when the meat is done, ah..." This was a lesson he learned from his ancestors and one he taught to his children.

I loved listening to the slow rhythm of his voice, something I learned to enjoy thoroughly in all the native communities I crossed. It's like no other accent I have ever heard and is mixed in with a lot of "ahs."

One moose would feed his family of four for a full year. "We depend on the fish we catch and the animals we harvest and trap to survive. It has been this way since the beginning, ah." Darcy explained how important it is in his culture to respect the wildlife that inhabit this great land. To his people, it is the only way to ensure a sustainable future.

On our second day resting at the Dewhurst's, I received a visit from a cowboy I look up to very much. "Filipe! How is the journey going so far?" Dana Peers, president of the Calgary Stampede, shook my hand. Along with Jason Coxford, Mike Little, and Ian Lister, he flew up to the Yukon to film a video on my Long Ride for the 2020 Calgary Stampede.

"I love your story and can't wait to help you share it at next year's rodeo," Dana said while the guys set up the equipment. I'd first met Dana briefly in 2012 before I rode out of the Centennial Stampede. His soft voice, big smile, and humble demeanor made me like him right away. In 2018, when I released my second book at the Stampede, I gave him a copy, and in the dedication, I invited him to ride with me during this final journey.

Dear Dana Peers,
Thank you for all of the work you do in promoting our Western culture. I look forward to seeing you in 2020 when I ride in for the Stampede from Alaska! If you want to ride with me, just let me know. I have a horse for you.

DANA TOOK me up on it, but never in my wildest dreams, did I imagine what would come next! While filming the video of us meeting up next to the Teslin Lake, Dana asked me a question that few men and women have been asked, "We want to celebrate with you, and I can't think of a better way to celebrate than to have you lead the 2020 Calgary Stampede Parade."

I was flabbergasted. "Wait, you want me to be the marshal?"

"Absolutely," Dana said as we hugged.

I couldn't believe it. This would be one of the biggest honors of my life. Past marshals have been Prime Minister Pierre Trudeau, astronaut Chris Hadfield, actor William Shatner, Canadian singer-songwriter Ian Tyson, Walt Disney, Olympians, and other prominent figures. When I started planning this Last Long Ride, I knew there was something calling me to Calgary. I didn't know what it was, but something told me I needed to undergo this final chapter. To receive this invitation made me feel like it was meant to be!

I had yet to find out my parade would be the first one canceled in more than 100 years.

BEFORE LEAVING THE DEWHURSTS, Clara and I went to the Teslin Tlingit Heritage Centre. We learned about this small community's history in a beautiful building with intricate native art and tall totem poles outside.

An elderly man who fell in love with my cowboy hat told us, "The community was first settled in the mid-nineteenth century by Coastal Tlingit traders."

Outside the large center, a group from the community was smoking some recently caught whitefish on the shores of Teslin Lake. I approached the group with my video camera, and they were kind enough to show me how they preserved the fish for the long winter months.

"After we smoke the fish in this hut, we use a machine to vacuum-pack the fillets," a young man in his early teens explained. It was an interesting mixture of their long heritage joined with new technology.

After filming the process, they invited Clara and me to eat lunch with them. Sitting in a circle, we enjoyed the fresh fish while we watched the hungry seagulls nearby fight for the leftover fish heads and guts. While we discussed how happy the birds were for the feeding, one woman told us her people used to eat seagull eggs when she was a little girl.

"Wow! Do they taste good?" I asked, interested in the story.

She didn't like my question. "Do you think my people would eat it if it tasted badly?" she shot back with fire in her eyes.

I apologized and felt extremely embarrassed. I didn't mean to say something disrespectful. I was honestly interested.

Luckily, another member of the community, noticing my embarrassment, spoke up. "Not everyone likes chocolate. I don't like them." He flashed me a smile which made me feel a little better and took the tension out of the awkward moment. After we finished lunch, we thanked them and left.

From the Dewhurst's quaint log cabin, we rode to the longest bridge in the Yukon. The challenge that had kept me awake at night for months awaited: the Teslin River Bridge, a 446.95-meter-long cantilevered bridge.

Since I first crossed it two months before while driving north, I wondered how the hell I would get my two wild horses to cross this beast's terrifying metal-mesh deck. Horses hate seeing through the surface they have to walk on and despise hearing loud noises when their feet touch the ground. That's exactly what would happen if we were to walk across. Now, here I was, standing only a few feet from this metal monster. There was no turning back.

In preparation for this moment, I purchased some rubber placemats along with four rolls of duct tape from the Fairbanks Walmart. Using a doll-sized pair of craft scissors, I cut the placemats to the same size as the horses hooves, and with the duct tape, I fastened them under their shoes like booties. I knew they wouldn't last the nearly half a kilometer, but I just needed them to muffle the sound of that first step onto the metal deck. That's if I could get them to take that first step.

I placed my hand in my right pocket and felt the small square tinfoil full of ashes Lisa had given me the morning I left her home. It was the size of a one-dollar coin. Her words entered my mind. "In our culture, we use the ashes from our fireplace to keep us safe and give us good luck," she said before she gave me the little package outside her log cabin.

With my eyes closed, I was transported to my first journey when I carried the ashes of Naomi Lisker from Craig, Colorado, to my home in Brazil. The young adventurer and horsewoman, who passed away a few months before I arrived at her brother's house, became a guardian angel for me on that first Long Ride. There were so many moments on that journey where I thought I was going to die or lose one of my horses. Somehow, we always came out alive on the other side. I genuinely believed Naomi kept us safe.

"Please help us get across this bridge safely," I whispered to the sky.

Hoping Naomi, wherever she may be, would hear my prayer, I took a deep breath and walked toward the metal monster. I led Mac, with Smokey close behind him. When I stepped onto the bridge, a drip of sweat ran down my spine. The big buckskin followed me onto the metal deck, but the small gray did not.

With his nostrils wide and snorting, I could see Smokey thinking to himself as he looked down at the wide Teslin River flowing with force beneath the mesh's square holes. *No, no, no! There's absolutely no way I'm walking on this thing!*

"C'mon, boys! Let's go!" I said, trying to get Smokey to step onto the bridge.

No luck.

I knew I didn't have much time. If he thought too much about it, we would never cross that bridge. I looked back and motioned for Lisa, who was helping us get across safely, to drive her white SUV closer to Smokey's hindquarters.

"C'mon, buddy, step on the bridge," I said in a soft voice while putting some pressure on his lead rope. When the car was about five feet from him, and with Mac already standing calmly on the bridge, the gray stepped forward. Without looking back, I marched.

In a few strides, the metal ate through the rubber placemats and the duct tape, and the noise the horses' shoes made hitting the deck was petrifying. Metal on metal! We sounded like a loud locomotive engine chugging away. It took us about ten minutes to get across the Teslin Bridge. When we finally stepped onto the other side, my shirt was glued to my back with sweat.

"*Yaaaaaahoooooooooooooooo!*" I celebrated. Another obstacle was now behind us.

14

SIGN POST FOREST

From Teslin, we followed fields full of the burning embers of bright pinkish-purple fireweed stretching high enough to touch the bottom of my stirrups. The flower, which became the Yukon's floral emblem in 1957, swayed with the wind under my boots.

"It's called fireweed because it's the first flower to grow in abundance after a fire clears a forest," an elderly gentleman with a wooden leg told me. He went on to warn me about a perennial tufted plant called foxtail. It looks beautiful, especially on a breezy day, but the bristles are barbed and will work their way into the eyes, nose, gums, and throats of animals, especially horses.

"Don't let them graze where there's too many," he warned.

Clara and I took his words to heart and would pull out all of the foxtail we found near the horses from that point on.

The stunning Cassiar Mountain Range made the ride dangerous and strenuous as we fought our way up and down the next few days alongside the Rancheria River. Bears continued to be a regular part of our days. We saw cubs, black bears, brown bears, grizzly bears, and mama bears. We even saw one black bear on the side of the road who had his front left paw cut off somehow. Luckily, none of these beautiful but petrifying animals bothered us.

On this desolate 260-kilometer stretch, we only found one corral for the horses to rest in. Luckily, it was six kilometers short of the halfway point. Continental Divide was a lodge, campground, restaurant, mechanical shop, and RV Park. It also had a corral for horses to rest in, a true miracle in the middle of the Yukon.

"I want to buy this horse," the basketball-player-sized owner of the establishment said before I even dismounted Mac.

"Sorry, sir, but he's not for sale," I responded as I climbed down, my knees and legs sore from days on the road. He tried to convince me the entire time I was there. Everyone always wanted to buy Mac and told me Smokey was a great woman's horse. I laughed it off, even when I was sitting on his back.

With the horses resting comfortably in the spacious corral and too much hay in front of them, Clara and I went to eat some real food at the restaurant.

As we walked in, a woman in her early fifties told us, "Sorry, we have no water in this building right now, so the restaurant is closed."

Feeling defeated, we returned to the horses. We decided we would do the next best thing: shower. When we went to try, there was water in that building, but no hot water.

We ate another plate of ramen noodles. Dirty and exhausted, I told Clara, "I just want to curl up in a ball and die."

The following day we rested. I wrote blogs. Clara studied.

The owner of Continental Divide continued to pester me about buying Mac. As we watched the big buckskin graze, he said, "I will treat him very well here. He will be a king."

I explained to him that, first of all, I needed to ride Mac to Calgary, and secondly, he was not my horse. "He was lent to me by a fellow Long Rider who wants him back," I explained, much to his dismay. He finally settled for a photo sitting atop the mighty wild horse.

When we went to pay for our time there, he didn't charge us anything. "You guys have a safe trip!"

I thanked him for his generosity, and we hit the road again, still dirty. The hot water never worked.

On the third day back on the road, I lost the horses next to the Alaska Highway once again. This time, it was due to a trucker who honked right as he passed Mac and Smokey. Riding Smokey, I lost hold of Mac's lead rope, and he quickly passed us as we followed him at a full gallop.

"*Amorrrrrrr!*" is all I managed to yell as we passed the parked motorhome going 25 kilometers per hour.

Clara, startled, poked her head out the window, her face as white as if she had seen a ghost. Eventually, I managed to stop Smokey and grab Mac.

I was fuming. A car nearly hit Mac. Riding these wild horses was like riding a ticking time bomb. You knew it would go off eventually, you just never knew when or where. No one was hurt, but I wondered how long our luck would last. When would one of the horses cross the road right in front of a vehicle? When would I fall off and break something when the horses took off out of nowhere? Or get my foot caught in the stirrup and have my body dragged for kilometers under one of the horses?

I was livid at my horses, but I was angrier with myself. This was all my fault. I hadn't had enough time to train them before beginning the journey. If something happened to these beautiful animals, it would be my fault and no one else's. That was the worst part.

ON THIS STRETCH, the tiny, annoying blackflies became a big problem. Trying to feed on our blood, they ate at the horses' skin and our skin all day. Humans and beasts were left with swollen wounds. It was hard to believe they came from such tiny insects. However, we crossed bridges, climbed mountains, bypassed bears, and survived the ruthless bugs, finally arriving in Watson Lake alive and well.

The night before riding into Watson Lake, Lisa and Darcy Dewhurst, our hosts from Teslin, came to camp with us.

Stepping out of her white SUV, Lisa said, "It's so nice to see you two again." Lisa's cousin John and his wife, who live on Vancouver Island and were traveling north with their motorhome-bus, also joined us. We camped out next to a creek about twelve kilometers north of town. With a small fire dancing between us, we drank and talked late into the night. It was a nice break from our lonesome ride during the previous two weeks.

The next morning, we bid our friends goodbye and continued on to Watson Lake. The rodeo grounds were located on the other side of town so we ended up arriving in the early afternoon.

"Welcome to the Watson Lake rodeo grounds," Rick Carter said when I finally arrived. I thanked him and began untacking Mac.

While I pulled the saddle off, his wife and granddaughter Olivia came to greet us as well. The eight-year-old girl immediately stole my heart with her questions about the horses and the ride. I tried to answer them as quickly as possible because there were so many.

After I turned my boys out in the huge arena in the center of the grounds, Olivia asked, "You want to see my horse?"

"I would love to," I responded with a smile. For the next hour, we tacked up her miniature horse, and I watched her ride in her bright pink boots and matching pink checkered shirt. She was too cute on that little pony. Clara and I couldn't get enough of it.

After she finished riding, she told us why she loved horses so much. "They're big and fast and probably the coolest creatures," Olivia said as she took the saddle off her pony.

After two weeks of ramen noodles, we drove to town eager to eat some real food. Rick Carter, who ran the rodeo grounds, invited us to dinner at his house the following day. We accepted happily. After two weeks in the middle of the Yukon wilderness, only seeing bears and trees, it was nice to finally be in a real town again, staying with a real family.

"I hope you two like homemade spaghetti with meatballs," the matriarch of the family said, making me drool. During the delicious dinner, Rick told us about how fate brought him to this small town thirty-three years previously.

"I was a truck driver for many years, and I used to haul cargo up north to Alaska. On one of my trips, my truck broke down and I never left," he said.

Everyone laughed at that.

The next day, Clara and I went to see the famous Sign Post Forest in the middle of the small town. Boasting 80,000 signs from all over the world, the "forest" is Watson Lake's most famous attraction. It all started during the building of the Alaska Highway in 1942 with an American soldier named Carl K. Lindley. While recuperating in Watson Lake from an injury, he was ordered by his commanding officer to repair and erect the directional signposts in town. As he was doing so, Lindley added his own sign indicating the direction and mileage to his hometown of Danville, Illinois. Soon, other soldiers were adding signs similar to Lindley's. The forest was born. It became a tradition, and travelers from all corners of the globe still put up signs from their home countries and towns.

"Wow, look at this one from China," Clara said, pointing at a blue rectangular sign with Chinese writing. It's an amazing experience to wander through the forest and see all the different signs and where they are from! Some were real signs from cities, states, and provinces while others were homemade. My favorites were a toilet seat, a bra, and a canoe paddle, all with messages.

Obviously, we had to leave our mark in the forest. Clara and I used the back of a license plate we found on the side of the road weeks earlier to write this message:

#JOURNEYAMERICA – *Alaska to Argentina on Horseback. 2012–2020. 27,000 kilometers. 12 countries. 564 horseshoes.*

WE USED horseshoe nails to fasten it to a thick pole. We also included a used horseshoe from the journey and a feather I found in the northern part of the Yukon territory.

"Looks good," I announced as we proudly gazed upon the forest's new addition. After two days' rest in Watson Lake, eating too much greasy food, and taking several warm showers, we were ready to continue trekking south.

I was excited to enter British Columbia, but I knew this would be the hardest stretch of the entire ride. South of Watson Lake, we would cross a 200-kilometer stretch of the Alaska Highway with several herds of massive wood bison, the northern Rocky Mountains, and one of the largest populations of black bears in the world.

15

WE ENTER BRITISH COLUMBIA

I rode out of the Watson Lake rodeo grounds on a warm August morning with Mac and Smokey feeling too good from their three days off. As soon as we made it past the gates, Smokey tried to take off bucking when Mac's lead rope grazed his back end.

"Shit!" is all I got out before I let go of Mac's lead rope and focused on staying on. He crow-hopped and tried to run off into the bushes. Luckily, I managed to get his head turned before he really got to bucking. I got off, walked back to where Mac was now grazing, and regrouped. It was at this moment that I witnessed something I had never seen before in my life. While I walked up to Mac, I saw him shoot his head up and turn it on an angle so his right eye was looking up at the sky. I found his reaction super weird, but when I looked up, I noticed there was an airplane flying low overhead.

"Mac, are you looking at that plane?" I said, not believing what I was witnessing. I didn't accept it then, but after paying attention to the large buckskin every time an airplane flew by, I confirmed it! Mac was the first horse I have ever met who enjoyed looking up at the flying machines. I just wish I knew what he was thinking. Maybe he wanted to fly.

A few kilometers down the Alaska Highway, we entered the province of British Columbia. Next to the tall "Welcome to British Columbia, The Best Place on Earth" sign with Mac and Smokey, I smiled wide for a photo. It's unbelievable how much energy these moments give while on a Long Ride.

"Only two more provinces and we are done," Clara said before I continued south. We were now out of the "true north." When we crossed the imaginary line that separates the Yukon Territory from the province of British Columbia, we also left the 60th parallel. I was one happy cowboy!

A few kilometers south, we received an unexpected welcome. Members of the Kaska Dena Council came to the entrance of the small town of Lower Post to greet us and offer many gifts.

"They filled our tank and all of the jerry cans with gasoline, gave us a bunch of groceries, and this cool hoodie for me," Clara said with a big smile. Only one day before her twenty-fifth birthday, it was as if the Universe wanted her to have these gifts.

The following evening, we were back on the Yukon and British Columbia border. That section of the Alaska Highway snakes its way back and forth between the territory and the province. We celebrated. Smokey and I were in British Columbia, and Clara and Mac were in the Yukon. As we enjoyed colorful cupcakes, the horses munched on their alfalfa cubes. All four of us wore rainbow happy birthday party hats.

"I love you, Clarita! Happy birthday," I said before we shared a long sugary kiss.

Having Clara out there with me made this Last Long Ride a million times better. Waking up next to her beautiful smile. Eating the delicious lunches she prepared, even though we didn't have a fridge. Going to sleep and snuggling together. I felt so blessed to have ridden to her home in Patagonia and met this angel who changed my life. And it was all thanks to the horse.

"*Te amo sabes*," I whispered to my *flor del pago*. I love you. You know that?

The horses stared at the motorhome with curious eyes as it rocked the night away.

The next morning, full of sugar and love, we entered the northern Rocky Mountains and everything changed. The highway, sandwiched between the Liard River and jagged rock faces, made the ride extremely dangerous. Motorhomes and transport trucks roared by, at times missing us by mere inches. The ride became hell.

However, the traffic and lack of space became the least of my worries. We had much bigger problems all around us. To be exact, eleven feet long, 6.59 feet tall, and 1,179 kilograms (2,600 pounds) in weight. On this section of the journey, we were forced to ride by several herds of wood bison. These beasts, armed with sharp horns atop their giant, fluffy heads, are extremely territorial. I held my breath and kept a tight grip on the reins every time I crossed their paths.

The big males always kept their eyes on the horses and me while the calves ran off into the woods with their mothers. Smokey and Mac snorted and tried to run off every time as I fought to hold them back.

Luckily, we never got chased, but the large male from the final herd we crossed began pawing at the dirt and took out his frustrations on a nearby spruce tree. He rammed it with his head repeatedly. I was sure glad it wasn't my body or the horses. The tree shook with its powerful blows! Green needles rained down on his head. During this stretch, I saw many willows and spruces snapped in half by other frustrated bison.

After 200 kilometers in bison territory, we arrived at the Liard Hot Springs Provincial Park. "Finally!" Clara announced as we untacked the horses in the campground in front of the hot springs.

We had heard about this warm natural pool of water for months. Almost everyone we met on the Alaska Highway traveling north raved about how we had to stop there for a few days. We told them we knew about the renowned hot springs, but we still had months before we arrived. Finally, as Clara said, we'd made it!

When I returned to the motorhome after getting the horses comfy in their high line and feeding them a mountain of hay, I saw Clara was boiling something in one of our two pans. We had just eaten, so I was confused. As she changed her clothes, I opened the lid to inspect what she was cooking. Shocked, I couldn't believe what I saw in the pan. Clara was boiling her menstrual cup to clean it out.

A menstrual cup is a type of reusable small, flexible funnel-shaped cup made of rubber or silicone that women use as an eco-friendly alternative to tampons.

I didn't know if I should puke first or start yelling. I couldn't believe it. We had only two pans. They were supposed to be for cooking our dinner. And now, we had obviously lost one to a menstrual cup.

"Clara, are you kidding me?" I fumed as I walked toward her.

"What's wrong?" she protested, not understanding my anger.

"What's wrong? What's wrong? You're boiling your dirty menstrual cup in our pan," I shot back.

"I cleaned it prior, Filipe, and I haven't used it in months. I don't have tampons, and I'm on my period. How do you expect me to go into the hot springs?" she said, now crying.

Looking back, I now realize I was wrong and insensitive at that moment. This girl was saving my life out there every single day. She kept me and my horses safe driving this motorhome through some of the most desolate places on earth. Here I was yelling at her, while she was in pain and bleeding, for boiling a clean menstrual cup in order to disinfect it. But at that moment, the macho man in me took over and all hell broke loose.

She yelled. I yelled. She cried. The pan was ruined, and so was our mood. I stormed out of the motorhome and went to hang out with the horses where, in a few minutes, Mac and Smokey agreed that I was a complete moron! I made my way back to apologize.

"I'm sorry, *amor*! It's okay, we'll just get a new pan," I said, trying to make up.

"Next time, try to be more sensitive. *I'm* sensitive right now, being on my cycle," she said before we kissed, made up, and finally went to take a dip in the world famous Liard Hot Springs.

As it turned out, we wouldn't have another choice since Clara chucked the pan under the motorhome and forgot about it. When she went to drive out a few days later, she ran over it and flattened it like a pancake.

The best part about my relationship with Clara is that we hardly ever fight, and when we do, we make up in minutes. Neither one of us hold grudges, and we forget about problems quickly.

Clara and I soaked our stresses away in the natural hot springs while the horses rested nearby. It was a beautiful pond in the middle of the forest. The water went from extremely hot near the spring to lukewarm the farther you got from it.

"Can we just stay here forever?" Clara asked.

"I like it! We can just boil your menstrual cups in the hot spring so we don't ruin any more pans."

I laughed.

She didn't think it was funny.

"Too soon?" I asked.

Definitely. Too soon.

On our way back to the horses, we met a wonderful family who gave us a $100 donation for the Barretos Children's Cancer Hospital.

"You guys have inspired us with your story," Shannon Moleski said as she passed me five $20 bills. "You are so young and doing something so beautiful."

They also gifted us a delicious grayling they'd caught the day before. We thanked them and cooked the delicious fish for dinner.

The following day we found an old corral a few kilometers farther south and after releasing the horses, went back to the hot springs. This time, tragedy sprayed itself on me in the form of pepper spray. When I went to put our knapsack in a wooden locker in front of the hot spring, the pepper spray can hit the shelf and let out a quick blast.

I shouted curses as I ran off with the backpack. I was worried the bear spray was going to choke all of the tourists bathing there. They would kill me for ruining their vacation. By the time I arrived back at the motorhome, my arm and feet were burning badly. I couldn't believe how strong the spray was. Only a little bit had gotten on me, and it felt like I had dropped hot lava on my skin.

I washed the affected areas with cold water for a few minutes and made my way back without the backpack. Feeling ashamed and still worried everyone at the hot spring was coughing their lungs out due to my stupidity, I ran into two women on the trail. They were coming from the springs talking about how bad it was.

I stopped them in their tracks and began to apologize. "Is it that bad back there?" I asked.

"Oh, yeah, it's terrible," one of them said.

"I'm so sorry, it was an accident. I was trying to put our backpack in the — "

The other lady interrupted me before I could finish, "Wait, what are you talking about?"

"The pepper spray. Aren't you talking about how it's hard to breathe?" I asked.

"No, no! We're talking about the two teenagers making out in the middle of the hot spring, practically humping each other!" She laughed.

"Wow, that's funny! I thought everyone was mad at me!"

We went our separate ways, laughing. When I got back, Clara was relaxing in the water along with tourists from all over Canada. She told me no one noticed anything, and I was the only one hurt in the accident. Due to my already burning skin, I couldn't stay in the hot water for long, so we called it a day.

The next morning, relaxed and with our skin feeling silky smooth from the sulfur, my feet and arm were still burning. We continued the tense ride south through the Rockies, fighting our way around every blind turn.

A few hours into the day, we rode by the vigil made for the couple who were murdered on the side of the Alaska Highway a few weeks previously.

"It's so sad," I told Clara when we met up a few meters down the road. "There are flowers, teddy bears, and an American and an Australian flag."

At this point, the teen murderers had been found dead in Manitoba where they committed a double suicide. Being at the crime scene and imagining what the young couple went through in their last seconds alive really hit home.

The killers drove south from Whitehorse before the murder took place. They must have passed us on the road at some point. "It could have been us," I told Clara.

Why did they pick an old blue van and not our motorhome? Or my horses? As I rode on that afternoon, a dark energy haunted me.

Two days after leaving Liard, we faced our greatest challenge yet, the rock-cut around Muncho Lake. The jade-green lake's name means "big water" in the Kaska language. It is flanked by stunning mountains that stretch far into the clouds and are mirrored in its serene waters.

I wish I could have marveled at the majestic scene, but the twelve kilometers of Alaska Highway, sandwiched between a jagged rock face and the lake, kept me moving. Clara stayed behind me and pleaded for trucks and cars to slow down.

On one of the worst stretches, a terrible blind corner with absolutely no space, Clara drove the motorhome behind the horses and me with the blinkers on. When we finished the corner, a truck hauling an RV pulled out from behind Clara and punched the gas right when it reached the horses.

The sound of the roaring engine sent my horses off into their usual adrenaline-fueled gallop. I fought to stop them as the RV passed us followed by another vehicle. For a second, I thought it was all over.

Once we left the danger zone, Clara complained, "People don't have a minute to slow down, to wait?" I shared her frustration, and it took me some time to get my breath back.

During this tense stretch, Clara also crashed the drone into some trees on top of the mountain while filming my progress. She came crying to let me know, thinking she had lost the drone forever.

"I'm so sorry," she said with tears running down her beautiful face.

"It's okay, don't worry." I gave her a hug. Luckily, the camera never stopped filming. I was able to walk back, climb the mountain, and locate the drone.

As hard as the past weeks were, nothing could have prepared us for what was yet to come.

16

SUMMER SNOW

On August 17, just thirty kilometers before arriving in Toad River, the rain which had fallen for days got heavier. The wind picked up, and the temperature dropped drastically. After yet another long day in the saddle, I decided to put the blankets Betty had given me in Tok on the horses. I was afraid of what the night might bring.

Mac stood perfectly still while I fastened his blanket, but when it came time to put Smokey's on, we had a rodeo. He tried to run off. He bucked. He cut my finger. He trampled the video camera and broke my tripod. After an hour, a lot of sweat, and a few drops of blood — my blood — he paced. He was so stubborn. His ears flattened, pointing towards his hind end, but the blanket covered his body.

Out of breath, I gave him a few pats on the neck. "You'll thank me at midnight tonight, kid!"

Just after dinner, what I was hoping wouldn't happen, happened. It started to snow.

"Welcome to a typical Canadian summer," I said to Clara, trying to lighten the heavy mood. A few seconds later, a glass fell from the table in the motorhome and shattered on the floor. Clara and I looked at one another. No one had touched it.

"Did that glass just commit suicide?" Clara asked.

"Wow! If my mom were here, she would say the devil is on the loose right now," I said.

The truth is, the energy was very heavy, the kind that makes you feel like a tragedy is near. It's the sort of thing that makes the hair on your neck stand up and the pit of your stomach twist. Maybe it was the barometric pressure, the heavy wind, or the snow in midsummer. Clara and I could both feel this foreboding energy pressing down on us.

I checked on the boys one last time and gave them more hay to help create warmth. Just before climbing into bed, it happened. Like a release, this energy we had been feeling blew up.

First, we heard a terrible explosion, followed by another. Then, for what seemed like a lifetime, came the deafening sound of metal scraping on asphalt. The horses panicked. We were parked on the side of the road, and it sounded like some out-of-control vehicle was coming right for our motorhome. Clara and I both braced for impact.

When the world went silent again, we looked at one another confused.

"Oh, my ! Someone just got into a terrible accident," Clara said.

I ran out. Clara tended to our petrified horses. I found a truck hauling a trailer, fifty yards down the highway. Two of its tires were blown.

"Are you okay?" I asked a blond young man in his early twenties. He looked like a surfer.

"Yes, yes, I'm fine," he responded with both his hands on his head in disbelief. The truck was sitting half on the road and half in the ditch. The young man looked like he was high on some kind of drug, or maybe he was just in shock.

"I need to get out of this ditch," he said, putting the truck into drive. He pressed down hard on the gas and tried to move the truck for a few seconds before giving up.

Outside analyzing the damage, he asked, "Can you pull me out with your motorhome?"

Luckily, an elderly fellow in a pickup truck was driving by at that moment, and he offered to help. They managed to get the truck and trailer back onto the road. The young man drove the rig slowly away with two rims scraping on the black, wet pavement. Sparks flew as he made his way south in the darkness of the cold night.

"That guy is insane," I concluded to Clara when I returned to the motorhome, nearly frozen. The snow was already piling up atop the grass next to the road. We tried to sleep that night, but it was a poor effort.

The next morning, we awoke to a winter wonderland. More than a foot of snow blanketed the world around us. Mac and Smokey stood under tall spruce trees, nice and cozy thanks to their blankets.

I was amazed at how warm the area actually was. Due to their size, the massive amount of hay I gave them, and the fact I tied them close together, they had created a microclimate under those trees that felt almost humid, like a rainforest. The snow had melted around them. Outside that little microclimate, it was bitterly cold.

With the thermometer reading -4 degrees Celsius and my crocodile-skin cowboy boots buried deep in the snow, I saddled up Mac. We started the most painful day of this third and final Long Ride.

"Drive safe, please," I implored Clara, who was still getting used to driving the bus-sized motorhome.

"I'll be fine. You be safe out there, please, *amor*," she said.

When I jumped into the leather saddle, it felt like I was sitting on a giant block of ice. Large flakes of wet snow, carried by strong headwinds, slapped me in the face like wet gloves. I had to tip my cowboy hat down to protect my eyes. Acting on instinct, my wild horses just wanted to stop and turn their back ends to the snow. They could not understand why we were riding straight into this terrible storm.

Before looking back to see if any cars or trucks were coming, I said, "C'mon, boys! We need to get down from this mountain."

Aside from the terrible snowstorm, we also had to worry about the blind turns and narrow road. I was frozen in that saddle. Stiff, with my hands and feet burning in pain, I wondered what I was doing with my life. I questioned my decision to ever leave Calgary seven years previously, never mind Alaska a few months before.

"Not a very nice day to ride a horse," a woman driving from Alaska to the lower 48 yelled out of a white truck.

"No, ma'am, but I am riding for a Children's Cancer Hospital in Brazil. I can't stop."

She took a photo of me from the truck and drove off. A few meters down the road, I saw her red brake lights come on and watched the truck reverse towards me. "This is all we have in cash! Good luck!" The Alaskan passed me a crumpled American $20 bill.

I cried frozen tears. At that moment, I was transported thousands of kilometers south to my home country to that hospital where I met so many children and teens who were fighting for their lives with smiles on their faces. My mind took me back to one smile in particular.

"Oh, my God, I can't believe you are actually here," Ellen Cristina said after we shared a strong hug. Her hair was all gone, and a tumor the size of an orange stuck out of her neck wrapped in gauze. She wiped tears of joy from her face.

"I'm your fan, Ellen," I said to the seventeen-year-old, blue-eyed beauty. A friend who worked at the Barretos Children's Cancer Hospital called me one day and told me Ellen's story. She was a bright and happy teenager diagnosed with throat cancer a few years before. Unfortunately, she was in palliative care.

The doctor explained that Ellen's father worked at a ranch in northern Brazil, and the owner lent her my book. She fell in love with the story and shared her dream of meeting me with the healthcare professional. As soon as I heard the story, I agreed to drive to Barretos to surprise her.

Ellen showed me her fluffy teddy rabbit. "I named my bunny Filipe," she said. "He's my warrior."

"I think I look better as a bunny than in my human version," I said. Ellen and all the nurses and doctors laughed.

I spent a few hours talking to Ellen about life, my journeys, her love for horses, and her disease. She explained how she was at peace with what was about to happen because of her strong faith. She believed God was with her the entire time and she was ready for whatever He decided was best for her.

She told me her favorite adage, one that helped her deal with the long and painful treatment she has faced. "Never cross your arms in front of a challenge, for the most important person in the world died with his spread wide."

With Ellen's stunning blue eyes and wide smile warming my soul, I straightened my back and trotted my horses through the maelstrom of the terrible snowstorm.

A few kilometers before arriving in Toad River, a snowplow driver stopped to check if Clara, parked on the side of the road waiting for me, was okay. After she explained what we were up to on that snowy morning, he offered a place for us to stay and a corral for the boys in town.

Just an hour later, we were inside his mother's home with his entire family eating a warm bowl of soup. Mac and Smokey happily munched on a mountain of hay in a corral just outside the door.

"Toad River has a population of about forty people and more than 200 horses," Nathaniel Steward said from the other side of the table as I thawed. Due to its proximity to some of the best hunting areas in North America, Toad River is home to several large outfitters. Located in a gorgeous valley, surrounded by dramatic mountains, there are pastures filled with horses on both sides of the highway.

We enjoyed a day off with the Steward family while the snow slowly melted away. When we told them about how Clara was trying to slow down traffic on the tight stretches of highway without much luck, they helped us spray paint a sign for the back of the motorhome that read: *Caution Horses Ahead.*

They even gave us a slow/stop sign. "This should help you guys down the road," Nathaniel's father Mark said.

We spent most of our time there with Nathaniel's brother-in-law, also named Mark, and his family. An outfitter for three decades, his house looked like a wildlife museum. A massive brown bear was on display atop large boulders just behind the front door. The bear stood on three legs, and with his front right paw, he looked to be about to strike a badger who was growling at him. Next to the bear's right rear foot, there was a massive grizzly skull. Next to that sat a horned ram skull. Atop the display hanging on the wall were two beautiful ram heads. All the animals had been hunted by Mark or his wife and two kids, and each came with epic stories.

"We were out on one of the hunting camps, and my wife had a bear tag. This bear right here was trying to get into the camp, and she ended up shooting it eight yards off the cabin porch," he told me as we studied the great big bear and its sharp teeth and claws.

Mark was in his late forties, but his eyes and smile made him look nineteen. He had a wicked sense of humor that kept me laughing the entire time I was around him. "Three-quarters of a black fly's body is composed of teeth," said the funny man, testing how gullible Clara and I were.

All the best hunting spots in the area were only accessible by horseback, so Mark had his own string of sixteen animals. They lived in a pasture in front of his house.

"Some of these guys we get up here hunting have never been on a horse before, so I look for friendly animals." He went on to explain how he also liked big-boned horses with large feet for the mountains.

On our second night in Toad River, Mark and his wife prepared a special feast for us. "Black bear spaghetti Bolognese!" Mark announced with a proud smile on his face. "You're always better to eat the bear than to let it eat you!"

He went on to explain how this was a bear his son harvested the previous spring and it was delicious. It was one of the best pastas I have ever eaten.

"Oh, my God, this is so tasty," Clara said as we devoured two plates of pasta.

After dinner, Mark showed us a petrifying video, scarier than the movie *The Sixth Sense*. It was shaky and the image was terrible. It was on an old VHS tape he'd spent half an hour looking for. In it, his wife was filming a male grizzly in the distance while he commented in the background, his voice low, at a whisper. While the bear dug for roots, Mark was heard coughing, louder than he wanted to. Suddenly, the animal shot his head up and took off, charging right for the couple and their pack-string.

"Oh, my God!" was all that was heard before the camera dropped and continued to film the ground. Mark is heard grabbing his rifle. After a few seconds of shaking and panting, a huge explosion was followed by a muffled thump. The horses were heard whinnying and galloping off into the distance.

"It took us all day to find the horses, but at least I managed to get that son of a gun before he got us," Mark told me, reminiscing about the petrifying moment.

Clara and I, who were already extremely scared of these animals before watching this bear charging the couple, now realized just how quick they were. We exchanged nervous glances.

"I can't believe how fast that bear got to them," I told Clara later. She agreed. Little did we know, we were about to have our own run-in with not one, but two of these devils!

17

TWO GRIZZLIES, ZERO SPACE

With the snow all gone, we began our final push to cross the northern Rocky Mountains. Before we left Toad River, we received a warning from our host Nathaniel, "There are two male grizzlies just after Summit Lake. They are right on the side of the highway digging for roots and are not moving." He explained how he had neared them with the snowplow, yelled, and slammed on the horn, but they didn't budge. "They don't seem to be scared of anything."

Gulp.

I thanked him for the heads-up and thanked this wonderful family for their hospitality. It's amazing how fast you are adopted by families on journeys like mine. Everything is so intense, the suffering so deep. The loneliness is immense, but the love is so abundant. When you arrive in their homes, in mere minutes you become their family and they yours. However, like hundreds of times before, all I could do was thank them for their generosity and bid them farewell.

"Here, take this," the matriarch of the family said before passing us a bag full of homegrown veggies and a $100 donation to the Barretos Children's Cancer Hospital. We hugged goodbye, and on a chilly morning I began my ride out of Toad River right next to the airport. The runway sat adjacent to the highway.

Nathaniel's last-minute words of caution, along with the scene in Mark's homemade video kept playing out in my mind as I fought my way through the final 100 kilometers of the Northern Rockies.

There are two grizzlies just after Summit Lake. They are right on the side of the highway eating roots and are not moving. They don't seem to be scared of anything.

It was a gorgeous ride that put us in danger several times a day. The road offered no space for me and my boys. Although it didn't snow again, the weather remained chilly, and it rained on and off. We crossed the highest point of the Alaska Highway: Summit Lake at 1,295 meters (4,249 feet).

Two days later, sure enough, I came face to face with the two male grizzlies. I spat a curse. "What do we do now?"

From my saddle, I watched them dig for roots about sixty meters south. Unsure of what to do next, I tried to hold the horses still. They had yet to see or smell the bears. They just wanted to walk. We turned in circles for a minute while I considered my options.

Due to the narrow highway, there was no way I was going to risk trying to ride by the two grizzlies. The beasts would be a mere five meters from us if we continued down the road, way too close for comfort.

While I analyzed the situation, I saw that the North Tetsa River ran parallel to the highway, deep within its steep banks. The river was plagued with large boulders. To drop into it, I would have to ride the horses down the steep and deep bank, also full of large rocks. I knew it would be dangerous for the horses and me, but it was my only option. Risk the horses breaking a leg and or flipping on top of me, wedging my corpse between their heavy bodies and the sharp rocks or risk being eaten by a bear? That was the question!

After a few seconds of turning tight circles and contemplating my options, I said a prayer, and with a lick of the spurs, we were off. I pointed my horses to the riverbank, hoping the bears didn't see or smell my horses and that Mac and Smokey remained oblivious to the danger that lay ahead. It took some convincing to get Smokey to go down the rock precipice, but he did and Mac followed behind. After plunging into the frigid waters, the horses fought their way south in the middle of the river while I ducked in the saddle, hugging Smokey's neck. I kept praying that the bears, only a few meters to our left, did not see, hear, or smell us.

I will never forget the sound of the horses' hooves sinking into the water, sometimes as deep as their bellies, and hitting the large boulders beneath. It was petrifying.

"Please, God, stay away, please, God, stay away, please, God..." I whispered this prayer repeatedly while we made our escape, my knees shaking, my feet drenched. It was a scene fit for a Western movie.

Clara watched everything from the safety of the motorhome, petrified for us. To her left, two massive grizzlies. To her right, her boyfriend and two wild horses. "Once in a while, I could see your white hat stick up over the edge of the river bank. I was so nervous," she told me later.

When I felt like I was far enough from the beasts, about 400 meters south, I kicked the horses out of the river, over the bank, and back onto the side of the highway. When I looked back, one of the bears was standing on his hind legs, trying to smell us. I continued whispering my mantra, and when we finally turned a corner where they could no longer see us in the distance, I kicked the horses up to a gallop.

Riding for half a kilometer in that river may have kept us alive, but it also caused Smokey to lose one of his back shoes and loosen the other. Just two kilometers away from the grizzlies, I was forced to take out my shoeing tools and get to work. Under heavy rain, I managed to nail on a new shoe and reset the other before continuing south.

A few days later, against all odds, we rode into Fort Nelson. My body ached from my hair to my toes, but I felt more alive than ever. Only 450 kilometers remained of the Alaska Highway.

IN THE EARLY hours of August 30, a crisp and foggy morning, we rode out of Fort Nelson en route to Fort St. John. After crossing the small town of 3,366 people, we immediately encountered our first hurdle. The long bridge that crosses over the Muskwa River was covered with thick fog. Riding over it with Mac and Smokey was way too dangerous. The cars would not be able to see us until the last second.

I hobbled the boys in a field right before the bridge and waited for the fog to lift. While Clara and I watched the horses graze, an elderly gentleman from town came to chat and take photos.

"I saw you riding by this morning and was too curious to find out what was going on," he said before using his Canon camera to snap a few photos of the horses. He then went back to his car and pulled out two coffees and two bagels with cream cheese and tomato, our favorite treat.

"Wow, thank you very much!" Stunned, I asked, "How did you know we liked our bagels like this?"

"This is a very small town, son. The woman at Tim Hortons told me exactly what you ordered every morning for the past three days. She is also curious as to what you're doing, so after this, she asked me to go back there to tell her."

Like everyone we met, he could not believe I had ridden to his town from Fairbanks, Alaska. And when I told him I had already traveled from Calgary to Ushuaia, he nearly had a heart attack. "I can't believe it, son. You are so young and have already seen so much."

When the way was finally clear, I jumped on Smokey and, ponying Mac, began making my way onto the bridge. I was still nervous since the traffic was heavier than we had met so far. Luckily, right before we stepped onto the long structure, a police officer arrived to save the day.

"Where are you headed, cowboy?" he asked after slowing down his vehicle to a crawl.

"I'm riding to Calgary, sir. Do you mind helping us cross this bridge?" I asked shyly.

He was a little hesitant at first. Then he asked why I was riding. Once I told him it was for the Barretos Children's Cancer Hospital in Brazil, he turned his lights on and got us across safely.

During this stretch of our journey, we saw the largest number of black bears on the entire trip! Some days, we encountered as many as five, leaving the horses and me feeling uneasy.

A friendly stranger even warned us of how to survive a black bear attack. "With grizzly bears, you have to play dead, but with black bears you fight 'til the end," the avid hunter and fisherman told me on the side of the road one day.

Luckily, we never had to test this theory since the bears always ran off into the woods when they heard or saw us. Ironically, in this land plagued with large carnivorous beasts, it was a small rodent that gave us the most trouble.

Clara shook me at 5 a.m. "Filipe, wake up, wake up! There's something making noise in the kitchen."

Startled, I tried to understand what was happening. I still had one more hour of sleep before my alarm went off. What could be so important?

"Listen, listen!" She crawled to the end of the bed, trying to look into the kitchen.

"It's the horses moving outside. Go back to sleep, Clara," I pleaded.

"No, it's not. I'm looking at the horses right now, and they are sleeping, as still as statues! It's in here, Filipe, listen!" She got out of bed and slowly crept to the doorway to look at the kitchen sink. "It's a rat!" Clara yelled before jumping back under the covers.

"What? How did a rat get into the motorhome?" I got up to see for myself.

Sure enough, this alien-looking pack rat, gray and huge, stared at me from inside the sink with his ET-sized black eyes. His little hands, beige and brittle looking, ruffled a piece of butter wrapper while his Mickey-Mouse-sized ears moved back and forth.

"Yes, you were correct. There is a rat inside the motorhome," I announced before jumping back into the bed beside her.

We were trapped. To get out of the motorhome, we had to cross the small kitchen, now under the control of the colossal packrat of the north. I hate rats. So does Clara.

"What are we going to do now?" I asked. It was too late. The acrobatic twenty-five-year-old was halfway out the tiny bedroom window. She jumped out.

"I'll open all the doors, and you use the broom to shoo him out," she announced. Once outside, Mac and Smokey looked at her like I had the pack pat minutes earlier. I wished I was the one who got to open the doors. Shooing out the rat scared me.

I got dressed. Then, with our red broom in hand, I inched my way toward the kitchen. The sound coming from the sink made the rat sound more like a grizzly than a small rodent. When he saw me again, I had no time to react. He jumped out of the sink with the grace of an Olympic high diver. He disappeared under the clutter next to our portable corral which was stacked on the wall adjacent to the small dining room next to the kitchen.

From outside, Clara demanded answers. "Is he out? What's going on?"

"No, he's now M.I.A.," I replied.

Scared and unsure of what to do next, I used the broom to push everything on the floor through the side door. Feed plates, buckets, and horse blankets tumbled out onto the gravel.

Suddenly, Clara yelled, "He's out! He's out!"

I let out a sigh of relief.

That relief didn't last long. Kneeling on the ground, Clara announced, "Shit! He just ran under the motorhome and climbed onto the frame!"

We quickly put everything back into the motorhome and closed the doors. While we ate breakfast, we laughed at our chaotic morning and decided our rodent problem was behind us. "Once you start driving, if he is still hanging onto the frame, he'll jump off," I assured her.

I tacked up the boys and started yet another day in the saddle. With fall quickly approaching, the morning air was cool. I rode for about fifteen minutes before I watched Clara pass me. The motorhome swerved down the road, and she pulled over on the right side of the highway in front of us.

Oh dear, I thought to myself. *I know what this means.*

Yup! ET wanted to go home with us. Standing outside the motorhome, we looked in the windows trying to catch a glimpse of our Houdini.

"I started driving and suddenly heard a noise coming from the back. When I looked, I saw the pack rat scurrying across the floor," Clara told me.

"How the hell did he get back in?" I wondered. I inspected the motorhome for holes. It didn't take long to discover the wall was shifting out where the panels from our portable corral were secured. "And here is his doorway into our lives," I announced.

I closed the large gap using cardboard and duct tape, before beginning the search for the intruder. Once again, I managed to push the rat out of the motorhome, and once again, he jumped back onto the frame under the vehicle.

"If there's no other holes, he will not be able to enter our house this time. I think we're safe," I said, before saying goodbye to Clara. I jumped back on Mac and began ponying Smokey south. I felt sure our morning problem was finally behind us.

I was wrong.

This pack rat really did want to join our herd and travel south with us. I must give it to him, his focus and inability to give up was admirable. His determination led him to the engine. After a few seconds of driving, Clara heard the rat running around frantically under the hood.

Again, stopped on the side of the Alaska Highway, I wondered what to do next. We opened the hood and sure enough, there he was, sitting perched on the battery. His wide black eyes peered into my soul. His small, yet sharp nails looked like they could take down a full-grown human.

I grabbed my weapon of choice, the red broom, once again. It didn't work. He found a small nook to burrow himself into and was not budging. In between black rubber hoses, colorful wires and metal, I could see his whiskers and the rest of his face once in a while.

Then I had an idea. Water! I filled one of the horses' buckets and tossed it towards him. He closed his gigantic eyes and took the jet of cold water like a pro, not moving an inch. He was now clean, but he wasn't going anywhere. Unsure of what to do next and with the day wasting away, I decided it was time for the heavy artillery.

"I know what will get him to leave," I said walking into the motorhome. Standing a few meters from the hood, with both hands on my gun, I aimed the barrel right at my prey and pulled the trigger. A jet of pepper spray shot out forcefully, and the stream made contact with my target.

Clara and I stepped back quickly to avoid breathing in the powerful spray, but we could hear the pack rat going berserk. He ran around the hood, then went to the frame, the wheels, back to the hood, then back to the frame.

"I guess he doesn't like peppers, either," I said. "We have something in common."

It was now close to lunchtime as I tried to start my day for the third time. Luckily, we never saw the rat again after I shot him with pepper spray, a powerful weapon against rats and grizzlies. I just hoped I'd never have to test it on the latter.

In the bountiful heart of the northern autumn, we found ourselves on the banks of the Buckinghorse River. Just under 200 kilometers south of Fort Nelson, we were surrounded by bright yellow balsam poplar trees. Clara and I watched the horses graze while the river flowed rapidly next to us.

"This is too beautiful," Clara said, glowing like the trees all around us. Enjoying the crisp and refreshing air, we rode towards the town of Wonowon. Falling leaves danced in the wind like hundreds of butterflies. It was all too stunning, too perfect, until we entered the civilized world once again. As we got closer to Fort St. John, the quiet and serene Alaska Highway turned into a chaotic array of pickup trucks, transport trucks, tractors, and oil tankers. The roads became extremely dangerous with heavy traffic. We had entered oil country.

When we arrived in Wonowon, I learned how the town obtained its peculiar name. Formerly known as Blueberry, British Columbia, it changed its name in 1954 to avoid conflict with another similarly named community in the province. Since the town sits on Mile 101 — "one-oh-one" — of the Alaska Highway, it became Wonowon. Personally, I liked Blueberry better.

"We used to be a sleepy little town years back, but now with the oil and gas traffic, it feels more like a big city," our host, Wendy Fraser, told us. Wendy, a pie-making machine in her early seventies, went on to tell us about other changes the industry brought to their "sleepy little town."

"Due to the fracking in the area, we now have regular earthquakes like the 4.6 magnitude (earthquake) in 2015." The sweet elderly lady explained that prior to the oil and gas companies moving into her backyard, she had never felt the ground shake in her life. Wendy also touched upon the development and opportunity the industry brought to her town. New businesses, better infrastructure, a booming economy were just some of the plusses. It was a double-edged sword.

"Nothing is perfect," she concluded. Her husband, Ted Friesen, used to be a chuckwagon driver. Chuckwagon racing is a popular sport at Canadian rodeos, and we spent hours chatting about the sport he loved dearly as we perused old photos.

In this event, teams of four horses pull "pioneer" wagons around a track reaching speeds of close to sixty-five kilometers per hour. The driver is supported by two outriders, each racing individual thoroughbred horses that follow the chuckwagon. It is one of the most exciting horse events I have ever seen. At the Calgary Stampede, it's the Super Bowl of chuckwagon racing. Standing close to the track, you experience the three wagons and eighteen thoroughbreds running full tilt for the finish line. Their thundering hooves make the hairs rise on your arms and your heart kicks up into a full gallop in your chest. It's an unbelievable feeling!

Since these are retired racehorses, in the past animals have sustained fractured legs and have suffered heart attacks while running. This caused major wrecks due to their speed and the fact that all the animals are attached to the wagon and each other through a harness. Unfortunately, when one horse goes down, due to a heart attack, for instance, others may need to be put down due to the injuries sustained in the accident.

Some hold the perception that the sport just kills horses. Ted disagreed. "What people don't understand is that these horses are retired racehorses. Chuckwagon drivers give them an opportunity to continue running. That's what they love to do and what they were born to do." According to Ted, if it weren't for the chucks, these horses would be euthanized much earlier.

"I loved taking care of my horses and feeling the ground shake when I let them out in the pasture after a race. They always took off running and bucking," the sixty-one-year-old man said, looking out the window as if his herd were still there.

The retired driver spent hours showing us his many trophies and belt buckles. His wife wouldn't stop feeding us. Clara and I had a wonderful time getting to know Ted and Wendy. They were tremendous hosts.

On our way out of Wonowon, I rode by a burst sour-gas pipeline on the side of the road. The smell was rancid. About fifty workers in orange jumpsuits and a dozen large machines and tractors worked away trying to stop the leak. I wondered what effects this burst pipeline would have on the environment.

"Hold your breath, boys," I told the horses while we crossed the contaminated area.

After trekking 381 kilometers with only one day off, we rode into Fort St. John. With a population of 20,000 people, it was no easy task to cross the bustling city. Luckily, Mac and Smokey were champs, and we arrived at the Light Horse Association. There, we would finally enjoy a few days off.

After thanking and feeding Mac and Smokey, Clara and I headed to town to celebrate and wait for two special guests to arrive.

18

KAREN HARDY AND BLUE

The day before riding out of Fort St. John, Karen Hardy, my American mom who helped me tremendously during my first long ride from Calgary to Brazil, arrived! "It's so nice seeing you two," Karen said before we shared a hug.

During my first long ride, Karen rode with me in New Mexico and Texas. She hosted me for my first American Thanksgiving. She gave me Dude, a mustang from the Taos Pueblo tribe that she trained herself. As if all that wasn't enough, she even met us at the finish line in the Barretos rodeo in Brazil.

The tougher-than-nails cowgirl drove from Washington State to ride with us. "You're my son. I had to come up here to make sure you finished this journey safely," she said while we fed her horse Blue alongside Mac and Smokey.

Having her by my side to finish the northern part of the ride was comforting. On Sunday, September 15, I rode Mac and ponied Smokey while Karen rode Blue by my side. Having someone to talk to all day made everything less painful and easier. Blue's calm demeanor eased a little of my boys' wild spunk.

The only hard part was moving the support vehicles back and forth every day. We would leave Karen's truck and trailer where we started. At the end of the day, I would wait with the horses while Clara drove Karen back to the rig. After about half an hour, they would show up, and we would set up camp. This ended up costing us three times what we would have spent on fuel, but it was totally worth it.

With Karen there, Clara was also able to ride with me for the first time on the journey. "I love Mac so much, but he's so wide my legs are killing me," she said one afternoon while she rode the big buckskin down a gravel road. "How do you do it?"

"I learned to ignore the pain," I laughed. As we neared the end of my Last Long Ride, I was experiencing a lot of pain in my left groin. It hurt when I walked for long distances or spent too much time in the saddle. It was a consequence of riding Mac for months.

It took 11,000 soldiers and 16,000 civilians eight months to build the original Alaska Highway in 1942. Nearly a century later, we traveled the 2,237-kilometer highway in half that time. Exactly four months to the day after departing Fairbanks, Alaska, I rode my mighty wild horses into Dawson Creek, British Columbia, with Karen by my side.

"Wow, I can't believe we are here!" I told Karen as we trekked toward the rodeo grounds. "A couple months ago, this moment felt nearly impossible."

On a short break at a gas station at the edge of town, the mayor of Dawson Creek, Dale Bumstead, came to say hello. He'd read about my journey. "We are happy to have you here, Filipe. Take my card. If there's anything you need, feel free to ask," the friendly mayor said before giving me a firm handshake.

The funny thing is that a few kilometers prior to arriving in town, I changed shirts and cleaned myself up using wet wipes to freshen up, "In case the mayor comes to greet us," I'd said to Clara and Karen as we all laughed. What were the chances? Sure enough, he came. See, kids? Your words are more powerful than you think!

Dale gave us a history lesson at that gas station. "When the USA entered World War II, the government worried that Japan would follow the destruction of the U.S. Pacific fleet in Hawaii with an invasion of Alaska." According to the cordial mayor, plans to build a road to Alaska had never materialized due to the difficulty of the project.

He went on to explain that within a few weeks of the Pearl Harbor attack, President Franklin D. Roosevelt decided that plans for a highway to Alaska, which had been around since the Klondike Gold Rush in the 1890s, deserved re-examination.

"It's difficult to imagine road-building conditions any worse than those workers faced in 1942," Dale added. "They had to carve a route over the Canadian Rockies, through the Yukon Territory, all the way to remote military outposts in Alaska."

One recruitment notice from that time helped us understand what these men were up against:

> Men hired for this job will be required to work and live under the most extreme conditions imaginable. Temperatures will range from 90 degrees above zero to 70 degrees below zero. Men will have to fight swamps, rivers, ice, and cold. Mosquitoes, flies, and gnats will not only be annoying, but will cause bodily harm. If you are not prepared to work under these and similar conditions, do not apply.

THE LINE, "mosquitoes, flies, and gnats will not only be annoying, but will cause bodily harm," resonated all too well with Smokey, Mac, and me!

The earth was so swampy in places that road builders could only make progress by laboriously cutting trees and laying them down, side by side, to form a corduroy road. This was then covered with large quantities of both dirt and gravel.

But again, the Alaskan and Yukon mosquitoes (or bush bombers as the soldiers nicknamed them) proved far more troublesome than any enemy!

Colonel William M. Hoge was responsible for this mammoth undertaking. In an interview after the completion of the highway, he recalled, "You had to eat with your head net on. You would raise the head net, and by the time you got food on the spoon up to your mouth, it would be covered with mosquitoes."

I knew all too well what Colonel Hoge meant. I, too, suffered under the reign of the blood-thirsty bush bombers. Yet, even with all these challenges, we succeed in our missions! Posing under the kilometer zero marker in the center of town, I was all smiles. We had finally ridden the Alaska Highway in its entirety! We had completed the most arduous section of the ride and nearly finished part one.

Cold beers were in order!

ON OUR FINAL push of this first part of the journey, tragedy nearly struck. One morning while I rode alone, Karen had trailered ahead with Blue to rest the out-of-shape horse. Mac and Smokey nearly took off for the highway. I was sitting on Mac, daydreaming about arriving in Grande Prairie when, out of nowhere, the ticking time bomb went off. First, Mac took that first powerful stride, going from a calm walk to an out-of-control gallop. Smokey joined in.

Luckily, I managed to stop the horses immediately, but only a few meters from the busy highway. "Whoa! Whoa!" I yelled, pulling on the reins and Smokey's lead rope. Unfortunately, when I pulled on the reins to hold Mac, I tilted my head down and a strong gust of wind popped my cowboy hat off my head and flung it onto the road. I watched in slow motion as the white straw hat hit the asphalt with force and trickled its way towards the other side of the road. It never made it.

"Oh, that hurts," I said, squirming in the saddle as I watched a transport truck with what seemed like a hundred wheels run over my hat. It was a pancake before it continued its course to the other ditch.

With the pancake that was once a cowboy hat in hand, I said, "Wow! That could have been my head!"

Four days after arriving in Dawson Creek and finishing the Alaska Highway, Clara, Karen, and I rode into Grande Prairie,

Alberta. It was my final destination for 2019 and the final province I would cross on my Long Ride across the Americas.

Sitting atop Mac, watching Clara ride Smokey and letting the light but freezing rain wash my soul, I couldn't help but reflect on these past few months. I felt so proud of our team. Mac and Smokey came a long way from when we started this adventure. Having Clara ride into a major city on Smokey was a clear example of how much they had matured.

"I can't believe I'm riding the wild horse I watched you work with in Osoyoos before the ride," Clara said with a wide smile. "He was so unpredictable, I thought I would never get on his back."

She and Smokey had a connection that I loved watching grow. Clara was the real heroine of this journey. For the past 124 days, she was there carrying hay, water, and feed every single day for the horses. She slowed traffic around blind curves to keep us safe. She kept me company through those long, desolate stretches of nothing and always bathed me in love.

The truth is, without my Clara, I may not have survived the north. This was by far one of the hardest stretches of land I covered in all of the Americas. There were so many hurdles to cross that at times I felt as if I were literally a character in the video game *Red Dead Redemption,* running nearly impossible and very dangerous missions.

Unlike *Red Dead*, I only had one life, and the obstacles were beyond a gamer's imagination. Fanged bears, endless bison, territorial moose, hungry wolves, giant mountains, metal-grate-deck bridges, summer snowstorms, clouds of blackflies, horseflies, mosquitoes, and two Canadian serial killers. When I passed one level, there was another challenge just as arduous waiting for us to navigate. But somehow we did it!

From Grande Prairie, Karen trailered the boys south to Osoyoos, British Columbia. Clara and I made the drive in the motorhome. It was wonderful to see Aaron Stelkia again. Smokey's owner and a renowned horse trainer, he was instrumental to the success of this Last Long Ride.

"The horses look great!" he said while we enjoyed a delicious dinner in his home.

The next morning, I pulled Mac and Smokey's shoes, and we released them in a huge pasture by Aaron's house. I thanked them for the past four months. "Enjoy the winter off, you goofballs," I said, giving each a pat on the neck and taking in a final long whiff of their smell. I wanted to take a part of them with me.

These horses were so powerful, we'd covered 630 kilometers a month. That's nearly double what I used to ride with the other horses for my first two journeys. These wild horses are majestic beings like no other! Their resiliency, strength, and natural survival instincts make them a great horse for a Long Ride.

After watching the boys run around their new home in excitement, Clara and I drove to see Sara Turner at a restaurant in Kelowna. "You made it!" she yelled while we hugged.

I noticed something was off right away. Sara tried to make small talk and act like everything was okay, but I could tell something was bothering her. After two beers, she exploded. "I can't believe you wrote in the *Toronto Star* that the horses took off on you so many times! I helped you to promote the breed, not make them look bad!"

"I'm telling the truth, Sara. You want me to lie? I also wrote about how strong and powerful they are, and if you hadn't lied about the horses being cut and rideable before I arrived, we wouldn't be having this problem," I yelled back.

"Oh, and you writing you trained Smokey to ride. He was already trained when you arrived."

That comment made me boil. "Already trained? Are you kidding me? He dumped Aaron twice and tried to get me off his back every day while I was working with him. I have it all filmed, Sara!"

The entire restaurant was now watching the epic fight going down.

She went on to blame me for saying the horses were afraid of bears. According to her, they weren't. She said it was my fault they ran off when they heard motorcycles.

I yelled back that she was crazy, that she had lied to me.

It was bad. Finally, I paid my part of the bill and stormed out of the restaurant while she cried and tried to apologize. After everything I had been through the past few months, I never imagined this was the way I would be welcomed back by Sara.

I was very immature to start yelling and say the things I said to her. She was someone who helped me tremendously during my first Long Ride. I should never have raised my voice, but her words were hurtful. I was trying my best to please everyone involved with the project, and guess what? I had just finished crossing Alaska, the Yukon, and Northern British Columbia on horseback. To say I was a little tense and short-fused was an understatement.

Unfortunately, our relationship was never the same after this. However, I will never be able to properly thank Sara for everything she did for my horses and me over the years. From taking care of Bruiser during my first long ride through Honduras to finding Mac and Smokey for this final ride and trailering them up to Alaska, I have said this before: my path is lined with angels. Sara was one of them!

From the Okanagan Valley, we crossed the Rocky Mountains en route to Claresholm, Alberta, where another pair of angels lived.

Marie Aitken welcomed us at her ranch. "We are so proud of you two!"

"Marie, you and Rocky figuratively and literally saved my life," I told her. It was true! The motorhome allowed us to carry feed, water, supplements, shoes, and other important equipment for the horses' health. It offered a bed for me to sleep in. Several times, I hid behind the motorhome while crossing paths with grizzlies or bison. It kept the horses and me safe every single day.

After spending a few days at the ranch, Clara and I flew back to South America to work and wait for the Canadian winter to pass so we could finish the final stretch of my Last Long Ride. With temperatures reaching -50 degrees Celsius from December to March, and with my arrival in Calgary planned for the opening of the parade, July 3 of 2020, this was the first time I'd broken a ride into two parts.

On a sunny Wednesday afternoon, Clara and I boarded our Air

Canada plane feeling a sense of a job well done. However, the recent fight with Sara also left an extremely bitter taste in my mouth.

I tried to focus on the positives. We had just gone up against some of the toughest terrain, harshest weather, and most dangerous wildlife on the planet and survived to tell about it. The horses were healthy and in great shape. Clara and I were becoming an amazing team. It felt like the hard part was behind us. Little did we know the greatest challenge of our generation was yet to come.

19

COVID-19

Clara and I spent Christmas in Brazil with my parents and the New Year in Patagonia with her family. It was weird stopping in the middle of a Long Ride and returning home for several months. This was the first time I did this, but it was the only way. I kept myself busy with motivational talks, book signings, and various promotional events. The thought of only having 800 kilometers left to arrive in Calgary made me feel like the hard part was over!

We'd had brushes with bears, bison, the northern Rocky Mountains, the Yukon, and its helicopter-sized mosquitoes. There was nothing more to worry about.

In late February, Clara and I went on a trip to the beach with my family in the coastal town of Ubatuba, São Paulo. We spent four beautiful days basking in the sun and recharging our energies in the Atlantic Ocean before flying back to Canada to finish the ride.

While we enjoyed our vacation, we kept a close eye on the news. Every day, there was a new development about this virus they were calling Coronavirus. I heard about COVID-19 in the first days of the year. Early on, it felt like a problem only China would face. The virus was on the other side of the world, and we would never be affected by it. Or so we thought!

As the virus traveled from country to country around the globe, arriving in Brazil in the final days of February, we began to understand the magnitude of this disease. Then, on March 11, a few days after returning from the beach, the World Health Organization used the term global pandemic for the first time.

"What's a pandemic?" I remember researching online, trying to understand what was happening. Clara and I were organizing our things to fly back to Canada. Our flight was booked for Thursday, March 19. Seeing how quickly this contagion spread and how countries were beginning to go into complete lockdown was like nothing we had ever seen previously. The growing crisis made us question if we would be able to finish the ride.

Prime Minister Justin Trudeau announced at a press conference in Ottawa on Monday, March 16, "We will be denying entry into Canada people who are not Canadian citizens or permanent residents as of Wednesday, March 18."

Sitting in my messy room at my family's ranch in the rolling hills of Minas Gerais state in Brazil, the prime minister's words hit me like a horse kick to the gut. Our flight was set to arrive in Canada on March 20, two days after the border would be closed. I couldn't believe our luck or lack thereof. Having ridden more than 25,000 kilometers across the Americas during the past eight years through blizzards, droughts, and devastating fires, it now looked like the COVID-19 pandemic would stop me from riding the final 800 kilometers. Had I finally met my match?

With more than 200,000 people infected with the virus and 9,000 deaths and counting, the world was shutting down quickly. The economy was fractured. Layoffs had begun. When the press conference came to an end, I simply sat there in silence, staring off into the abyss of my uncertain future.

"How are we going to finish this ride?" I asked Clara. She had no answers and, at that moment, I had no hope. I knew my words were selfish, even petulant. However, like many times before during my rides, I knew that quitting was not an option.

For so many people along the way, the pursuit of my dream somehow became their dream. It's complicated to describe, but over and over the poorest people gave me their best, their kindness, and their hospitality. Although I had nothing to give back, they seemed to take inspiration, and even hope, from my journeys. As I pursued my dream, I gave them hope that they could pursue theirs, that anything was possible with hard work, focus, and dedication.

A Patagonian *gaucho* once said, "You aren't different or special. You are just a simple man facing his obstacles on the path to his dream, proving to others that they can face theirs. There's great power in that."

I had come too far to stop now. I had to find a way to enter Canada before the border closed for what could be days or months, or maybe even years. No one knew anything at that point.

That evening, a friend who knew about my situation texted me saying that the border closure only went into effect as of noon on Wednesday, March 18. After calling Air Canada, I found out there was a flight leaving São Paulo Tuesday evening and arrived in Toronto at 6 a.m. the following morning. It was my last chance to enter Canada. I needed to try to rebook. The only problem was that the flight was full.

With no Plan B, Clara and I threw our clothes into four suitcases that night. The following morning, we drove to São Paulo's Guarulhos Airport in a rental car desperate to get on that flight.

"See you tonight or in five months," I said, before giving my parents and sisters hugs. My father looked at me unhappily. He felt like I was making a big mistake in leaving Brazil at that moment and traveling to Canada. He thought I should stay put until we knew more about the virus and the pandemic. His dismay made me question my decision to go.

However, Clara, my rock, gave me the push I needed. "Filipe, if we don't try, we will never know what could have been. We may not get on that flight, but we need to try. If we get on, then it was meant to be."

When we arrived in Guarulhos, we were shocked at how quiet the normally bustling airport had become. Many of the travelers wore face masks and dishwashing gloves. Everyone had fear in their eyes. No one stood too close to each other, and when someone dared to cough, heads turned and eyes rolled.

We waited by the Air Canada counter for four tense hours as travelers checked into flight AC91. Finally, after the last passenger walked away from the counter, we were given the news that two passengers hadn't shown up so two seats were available. We couldn't believe our luck. With a sigh of relief, we checked our bags, had our hand sanitizer taken away at security, and entered the Boeing 787-9 aircraft. It was meant to be!

"Right foot first for good luck keeping this nasty virus out of this plane," a short lady in her sixties announced before she stepped onto the plane. I followed her on, right foot leading the way, as well. After a bumpy ten-hour flight, we landed at Toronto Pearson International Airport.

Much to my surprise, we were met with no tests or information on coronavirus. No fever checks, no questions on whether we had visited China or Italy in the past fourteen days, no pamphlets saying we should self-isolate.

Only a grumpy border agent questioned what we were doing traveling at this time. "Do you know what's going on right now?" the bald man asked Clara with a cold stare before disgustedly tossing her passport on the counter.

Of course, we knew. We were wearing masks and surgical gloves, entering Canada six hours before it closed its border to foreign travelers. We'd gambled on getting marooned thousands of kilometers away from our family and friends. In the middle of the worst pandemic of the twenty-first century, we certainly knew.

There were so many unanswered questions and fears at that moment. We didn't know when or if we would be able to return to our homes. We worried we would lose family to this virus. But like many times before on my journeys, I focused on staying positive and worrying only about what I could control. I had to get to my horses!

"We made it! I can't believe it," Clara said, still wearing her deep-blue mask when we finally stepped off our final flight in Calgary. Just like Guarulhos in São Paulo, Calgary International Airport's corridors stood empty. All the stores were closed. No seniors in white cowboy hats greeted us with big smiles saying, "Welcome home!"

But we had arrived. We exited the airport and staggered into freezing temperatures. We hugged to warm up. "Can you believe we were at the beach two weeks ago?"

Rocky Aitken drove up in his Ford pickup a few minutes later and drove us to his home in Claresholm where he and Marie were quarantining.

"I can't believe you guys got into the country," my Albertan mom said in disbelief when we entered her house. Once again, Rocky and Marie were saving our lives. While many people feared coming into contact with others, especially those who were traveling from a different country, they opened their doors to us.

With Alberta still under a heavy blanket of snow, we spent our days helping Rocky feed the horses at the ranch and drinking way too much coffee as we watched the news. Our plan was to spend our quarantine with the Aitkens before driving to Osoyoos to begin working with Mac and Smokey again. However, only three days after arriving, Dana Peers, the president of the Calgary Stampede, warned us that the provinces might close their borders.

After speaking to the Premier of Alberta, Jason Kenney, Dana warned, "If I were you guys, I would drive to the horses now and finish your quarantine in the motorhome."

We spoke to Marie and Rocky, and they agreed this would be the best plan. If the border between Alberta and British Columbia were to actually shut down, we wouldn't be able to get the horses in shape for the second part of the journey. That would put our arrival at the Calgary Stampede rodeo on July 3 in jeopardy.

With enough gas in jerry cans to get us to Osoyoos stocked in the motorhome and food for two weeks, we hugged Marie and

Rocky and began the drive over the Rocky Mountains. Not coming into contact with anyone and only stopping to sleep half-way (in the motorhome), we arrived in Osoyoos with a major problem. We had nowhere to park the motorhome to finish the quarantine. Because Aaron's mother was eighty-nine, he was afraid of welcoming us to the ranch before we ended our quarantine. Rightfully so!

Clara and I looked at Google maps hoping to find somewhere far away from the town where we could park the vehicle. We searched and searched until we finally found a conservation road that snaked its way up a mountain about ten kilometers outside of Osoyoos. "This is the only place. Let's hope we can park there," I said to her before we drove to the mountain.

We arrived in the early afternoon and after driving up the mountain for a few minutes, found a plateau to park the motorhome. It was a flat spot that had a bonfire ring made of large rocks. The spot featured a spectacular view of the valley below. It was the perfect place to spend the next two weeks. It was also the only place!

"I just hope no one calls the police on us," Clara said as we made ourselves at home.

This was a feeling that stayed with us the entire fourteen days we spent on the side of that mountain. The entire country was on lockdown. Businesses were shut. Most people were working from home. No one was traveling anywhere but to the supermarket.

We read news stories online of cars with Albertan license plates being scratched up in British Columbia. People were turning on one another. Fear will do that. We tried to stay positive.

Our days started just as they ended, with nothing to do. We went on long walks up and down the mountain, did sit-ups, and collected snow to shower. I started a podcast. Clara knitted. Quite honestly, it was one of the best two weeks of our lives.

"This place is gorgeous," Clara said to me as we drank *mate* tea one morning while the sun kissed our faces.

Three or four different cars would drive up the mountain every day and then back down. We wondered if one would stop to ask questions as to what we were doing there, where we were coming from, or who allowed us to park there for so many days. But they never did.

We did have one unwanted visitor, though! Clara awoke me in the middle of the night. "Filipe, there's something making noise in the kitchen!"

Deep in my heart, I knew who it was! ET's cousin from Northern British Columbia — another rat. "Why, God? Why?" I asked as I watched a smaller version of the first rodent who'd given us trouble a few months before running around the kitchen.

This time, we were not able to figure out how he entered the motorhome. Getting him out proved to be harder than the first time we had a pest problem! It took two full days to get rid of our unwanted visitor and two sleepless nights. Eventually, he left and our quarantine ended.

On day fourteen, we celebrated the end of our official quarantine by driving to the closest grocery store to stock up on food again. Then, just in case, we drove back up the mountain to spend an extra two days there. If we'd brought this virus to Aaron's mother, we would never be able to forgive ourselves.

Finally, on April 4, we arrived at Aaron's ranch in Osoyoos. We could hardly contain our excitement to see Mac and Smokey again. Although they had nearly killed me several times during the first part of the journey, I missed the two spirited horses.

When we walked up to them, both had their heads in a bale of hay. Burs were stuck all over their tails and manes.

"You guys are so dirty!" Clara said.

We at once got to work grooming our kids and getting them into riding shape. After the long Canadian winter, they were both fat and in need of exercise, but the important thing was that they were healthy and well-rested.

I first worked with Mac and Smokey in the round pen to see how they would act. After so many months off, I wasn't sure if they would try to buck or not. They worked great! We started riding them out on Aaron's many trails in the desert.

"This place is absolutely beautiful," I said to Clara on our first day out. The last time we were there training the horses, everything was so chaotic. Having to castrate and train Smokey and find a second horse, we really hadn't had time to enjoy Osoyoos. This time, it was different. We had at least a month to get the ponies into shape and really get to know Canada's only desert and its unique culture. The beautiful weather, much warmer than Alberta, also helped.

Everything was going to plan until April 23. The Calgary Stampede Rodeo, which had not missed a year since it became an annual event in 1912, was canceled — the first time in over 100 years!

"As a not-for-profit, we knew that any decision was going to be a larger decision about the community, about everybody that would be affected economically through this process. It was not a decision that we came by lightly," Dana Peers said, "but it is a decision that is in the best interest of public health and safety."

His words hit me like a wrecking ball. I didn't know what to say. I was at a loss for words. I just wanted to wake up from this nightmare. My plan was to start riding the final 800 kilometers I had left to cross in the Americas in May and arrive in Calgary on July 3, just in time for the Greatest Outdoor Show on Earth. Having ridden out of the Centennial Calgary Stampede Rodeo in 2012 on my first Long Ride, this was supposed to be my Disney ending. I was the 2020 Grand Marshal, a secret I had kept since July of the previous year and would now remain a secret forever.

However, I had bigger problems than sulking about the cancellation of my welcome home parade. With Alberta in lockdown, I wondered how I would be able to get my horses into the province and finish my cross-continental ride.

20

OSOYOOS

Our month in Osoyoos, British Columbia, was nothing short of wild! While we waited for the line on the COVID-19 infection graph to drop and Canada to reopen, Clara and I rode Mac and Smokey every day to get them into shape. We also helped master horseman Aaron Stelkia around the ranch.

Aaron, who lent me Smokey, was training several wild horses for a sale he was putting on in the summer with the help of Jessi Wyatt and her sister Thaleta, two cowgirls who grew up in the area. "I am hoping to give these wild horses a chance to go to good homes instead of straight to slaughter for meat," Aaron explained.

I watched him work with a wild pinto stud in the round pen. He had been doing this his entire life, and his experience was quickly evident. In a few minutes, the animals were already facing him and even following the cowboy.

"The first thing you want to teach them is to come to you," he said, lunging the beautiful pinto. Known as join-up, this is one of the most important moments in training a horse. It's that moment when the horse decides that it is better to be with the person than to go away.

What a difference one year can make in a person's life. The first time I met Aaron, he was out of riding shape. He hadn't worked with horses since the passing of his son. He had given up the life he knew to mourn. However, since Sara entered his life with this crazy project, the horse trainer had swung back into the saddle.

"It feels good to be working with horses again. I just hope the sale goes well, and we are able to recoup the investment we've made," Aaron said, donning a brand new salmon shirt and crisp straw hat. The change was clear. He smiled more and shaved regularly. He looked like he was sleeping better, playing fewer poker games until the wee hours of the morning. He spent his days training different horses in the round pen. It felt good to see this kind man who had been hit so hard by life making some positive changes.

While I helped put miles on some of the horses in training, I nearly broke my neck. During one ride, on a dark horse with the shifty eyes of a lunatic, I was telling a story to Jessi Wyatt. My body was turned around in the saddle and facing her. I slammed my chest with my right hand. I don't remember why the story required the chest slap, but as soon as I heard the thump, I knew I had made a mistake. In mere seconds, the world entered chaotic mode. I did a full front flip in the air before landing on my back.

Startled, Clara asked, "Oh, my God! Are you okay?"

"Yes, yes, I'm fine. I'm an idiot." I got my breath back as I walked back to my horse. The moment you relax on these wildies, especially while they are being trained, is the moment you eat a mouthful of dirt.

We didn't just work with horses at the ranch. Aaron and his family also ran about 400 head of cattle, and we arrived just in time for branding season. As a cowboy, I love these opportunities to help brand, castrate, and vaccinate calves. It's a tradition that has remained pretty much the same for hundreds of years, and after the work is done, there is always a feast.

"I made this soup this morning, so dig in," said Jane Stelkia, the recently turned ninety-year-old matriarch of the family. As she removed the lid from the large pot, the smell, a mixture of beef and potatoes, made me drool.

The work with the cattle took several days. After we finished, Jane invited us to her home to see artifacts she had found in the region over the years. Clara and I watched in awe as she showed us arrowheads, tomahawks, and animal bones – now turning to dust – that traced back hundreds of years.

"When I hold these, I feel even more connected to this place," Jane said with a big smile on her wrinkled face. She then went on to tell us about the importance of the horse for all First Nations people in Canada. "To the Indians, the horse was everything," said the oldest living member of the Osoyoos Indian Band.

Jane took out a handwritten speech she'd given a few years before when the band inaugurated a riding program to help inmates. It read as follows:

Good morning! My name is Jane Stelkia. I am the oldest member of the Osoyoos Indian Band. I will be 88 in a few months, born on April 11, 1930. I would like to thank the chief and council for asking me to be a part of this event today.

It's great to see programs like the horses being offered to prisoners now and hopefully more to come. This will help them learn compassion and respect. Being hands-on gives a person connection and an amazing experience.

In fact, hundreds of horses have roamed this valley and generations of these horses grazed right here, where we stand today.

To the Indians, the horse was our means of moving camps to different locations, hunting, fishing, berry picking, digging roots, traveling, racing, fun, and games.

The horse was even considered a babysitter for children of all ages, including babies.

So it's great to see horses being used today to help others gain the connection, responsibility, compassion, and respect for the horses and themselves.

AFTER TRAVELING BACK in time in Jane's living room, her daughter Dora took us on an adventure in the mountains. In her side-by-side vehicle, we crossed streams and climbed steep hills while she told us about this gorgeous land. Dora was blonde, had light eyes, and wore reading glasses. In her forties, she loved capturing the serene beauty of her surroundings with her camera. She was a true artist. A mother of two boys and one girl, she lived for her children and worried about them constantly.

"This is a pictograph from thousands of years back," Dora said while we looked at the work of art on a rock face. It was a rust-red color and showed a person hunting a deer. Looking at the painting made me travel back in time even more. I wondered who painted it and when.

It was like visiting Cueva de las Manos in Patagonia during my ride to Ushuaia a few years previously. At one point in our adventure, we were atop a hill surrounded by bright yellow sunflowers watching a herd of wild horses gallop away while a black bear climbed the ridge with her two cubs. I felt blessed to be a witness.

Osoyoos, located in the majestic Okanagan Valley, is one of the most beautiful places I have visited during my travels. The mountains, lakes, wildlife, native culture, flora, and people — I fell in love with it all!

"I love this place and wouldn't trade it for anywhere else in the world," Marie Stelkia, Aaron's other sister, said to Clara and me over dinner one night.

During our month training the horses, we also got the opportunity to meet Chief Clarence Louie. "You know I used to ride bulls when I was young and fit like you," the kind-eyed First Nations leader said to me inside his brand new community center. Colorful native art, black and white photos, different animal footprints on the cement floor, and a stunning oval meeting room were just some of the highlights.

Louie had been the chief of the Osoyoos Indian Band for ten terms, the first beginning in 1985. He is credited by many with the economic success of the small community, one of the richest native reserves in Canada.

"I love what I do. I love creating jobs," Louie told me. "I want to see my people working. I don't believe in welfare."

It's not only the members of the reserve who think the chief is doing a tremendous job leading his community. Louie received the Order of British Columbia in 2004 and the Order of Canada in 2016.

When I asked about the awards, he answered humbly, "I just need to worry about making my people happy."

I feel lucky to have spent as much time as I did in the Osoyoos Indian Band, with its members and horses. This land is magical. Smokey and Mac were born in this valley, and now, it seems like I am connected to it as well.

MY JOURNEY across the Americas would have been a lot harder, if not impossible, without the help of so many people. During the past eight years I had been welcomed into the homes of loving families from Fairbanks, Alaska to Ushuaia, Argentina. Nearly every night of the more than 1,500 I've spent trekking, people opened their doors to host me and my steeds. I had been given food, water, a bed, and presents without being asked for anything in return. I have said it many times before, and I'll say it again, one of the biggest lessons I have learned from this journey is that 99.9 percent of people are good. Great! From politicians to ranch hands to drug lords, it has been such a humbling experience to sit at the dinner table with people from all walks of life in the twelve nations I crossed.

One family in Guatemala butchered the only chicken they had, which they were saving for Christmas, just to feed me one night. I will never forget these acts of kindness and love. But, in this post-pandemic world, things had changed. People were fearful of one another.

As I prepared to begin the final stretch of my cross-continental ride, more than five million people had contracted the virus and

346,000 died. In many ways, our world would never be the same again, and the final 800 kilometers I rode in the Americas might look a lot different from the 26,000 already traveled. When Alberta finally began opening its parks again and coming out of lockdown, the first of what would be many, we decided it was time to go. It was now or never.

In Grande Prairie, Alberta, our starting point for this final stretch, we were unable to find a place to rest the horses prior to setting out. Friends from Calgary tried to find a ranch, farm, or riding facility that would take the horses in for a night or two. No luck.

"Sorry, Filipe, but everyone is really afraid of this thing," a Calgary Stampede volunteer who lived in the area told me over the phone.

The night before we started our ride to Calgary, Smokey and Mac stood munching on hay tied to trees on the side of Highway 40. Aaron Stelkia trailered them up, and we followed in the motor home. It was not the way I imagined I would start this final chapter of my Long Ride across the Americas, but it was a clear sign of the times.

That was one of the most interesting parts of this project. From the back of a horse, you get the truth about life, society, animals, people, and the land without the BS. As I prepared to begin, I wondered how people would react to Clara and me doing this at this challenging time. Was I putting our lives in harm's way? Others' lives? I didn't know if I was making the right decision or if it would come back to bite me in the ass, but I was following my heart. My instincts told me I needed to finish what I started almost a decade ago. So that's what I did.

21

THE FINAL STRETCH BEGINS

On Wednesday, May 20, I saddled Smokey just outside of Grande Prairie near the Wapiti River while a sparrow sang a lively song. A movie played out in my head. I was about to embark on the final stretch of my cross-continental journey, just over a month shy of celebrating the eight-year anniversary of my departure from the 2012 Calgary Stampede.

"I can't wait to live the life of a Long Rider for the final time," I said to the camera as Clara filmed me. My voice cracked. The faces of people who had been instrumental to our success popped into my head, and two of them stood nearby watching. Rocky and Marie Aitken, the couple who lent us the 1990 Econoline motorhome we were using as a support vehicle, allowed us to begin our quarantine in their homes. They'd adopted us and were there to see us off.

"We brought you Tim Hortons and Hawkins Cheezies, a real Canadian treat," Marie said, handing us the delicious presents with a warm smile on her pale face.

After my Canadian breakfast, I hugged them goodbye and mounted Smokey while ponying Mac. We took the first stride into the unknown. All the stress and anxiety from the previous months faded away. I felt like I could do this. With the reins in my hands, all the problems and fears brought on by the pandemic seemed far, far away. But like the beginning of all my journeys, tragedy nearly struck right away.

Right out of Grande Prairie, Highway 40 bustled with oil and gas traffic. As we tried to stay as far away from the road as possible, the horses found their way into a deep bog less than three kilometers from the starting point.

"Oh, shit!" I said as I felt my stirrups hit the mud, followed by loud suction sounds coming from the horses legs as they sank. I quickly jumped out of the saddle and began pulling Smokey's reins and Mac's lead rope while yelling, "C'mon, boys! Get out! Get out!"

Both horses fought their way out of the bog, and in a few seconds, everything went silent as the chaos ebbed. Only heavy breathing from man and beasts could be heard. Deep black mud stuck to their legs and bellies. Even on top of my saddle there were big mud spots. All three of us took a deep breath to recover before we continued south, but this would not be our last run-in with the mud.

That night, after riding twenty-five kilometers, we found refuge near a natural gas pipeline. There was tons of green grass for the horses to graze on, and a great spot for us to sleep. It was a wonderful night, but the next morning we awoke to rain and very quickly realized the motorhome was not getting out. The road we parked on had turned into a muddy mess. When we tried to back up the motorhome, she sank and she sank good.

As we tried to figure out what to do next, a white truck stopped.

"Maybe he can help us," Clara said.

With the pandemic raging, I questioned if the person in that truck would feel comfortable coming into contact with strangers. With no other options, I ran over in the rain. It turned out the Universe had sent us an angel. His name was Greg Wakefield. The plump man in his early fifties rolled down his window when he saw me standing outside his vehicle.

"Good morning, sir! I'm riding horseback to Calgary, and our support vehicle is stuck in the mud. Do you think you can help us get it out?"

"Oh, I'll get you guys out, no problem," Greg said before he moved his truck to the front of the motorhome. Turns out Greg was a bull rider back in the day who now worked in road construction. "I built the original Highway 40, and now I'm back expanding it," he told us with a big smile. In fifteen minutes, we hooked up the chain Greg carried around for this exact purpose, and with the rain still falling, finally pulled the motorhome free from the mud. We did it all while practicing social distancing. Not an easy job.

"Thank you so much, sir. You saved our lives," I said to him, before continuing, "I wish I could hug you!"

We all laughed. Seems like not even a pandemic could stop "trail angels," as the late, great Long Rider Bernice Ende — one of my mentors before I ever jumped into the saddle — used to call these helpful, heavenly folk.

THE ROAD to Grande Cache reminded me a lot of our time riding through the Yukon and Alaska. Muskeg began a few feet from the highway on both sides, and there were no ranches, farms, or towns in sight. Black spruce trees and raging rivers of all sizes dotted our course.

On our second day out from Grande Prairie, it started to rain, and it did not stop for three days. It was a cold and miserable ride as Smokey and Mac fought their way through the mud while oil and gas trucks flew down the road next to us. It was not a pleasurable experience, but like many times before, all I could do was put my head down and ride on.

My wild horses handled the first week back on the road extremely well. Thanks to the time we spent in Osoyoos getting them into shape, they were feeling great and looking great. With their muscles bulging, we trekked about twenty-five to thirty kilometers each day.

I also spent a lot of time working with getting them accustomed to the combustion of an engine. That noise always set them off into a galloping frenzy during the first part of our journey.

Using a chainsaw Aaron lent me, I would turn it on and off continuously several times a day, right behind the horses' back end. Sometimes I would feed them and then leave the chainsaw running behind both horses, pressing down the trigger and making the machine rev up every couple of seconds. So far, it seemed like it had helped them understand that engines were not predators!

On the third day out, I found a moose antler in the tall grass. I have found a lot of things on the side of the road these past eight years: money, license plates, underwear, shoes, and gloves, for instance. Moose antlers were a real treat! Having fallen off a young male, it had five points on it. Unfortunately, the top point had broken off, but other than that, it was intact. Holding it in my hand, heavy and thick, it was hard to believe they grow these every year only to shed them again.

Apparently, this wasn't just moose territory. While chatting with a friendly stranger who worked for an oil company, I was told to be careful of the grizzlies. "This area you are crossing has the largest number of grizzly bears in the world," he said, sitting atop his ATV next to the road.

"Are you sure? Because I think there are more in the Yukon." I explained how many bears we had seen the previous year, at certain points, three bears in a day. He didn't buy it.

Luckily, we never saw any bears, but did get warned once that there was a large grizzly sow with two cubs a few kilometers ahead. Thankfully, they were gone by the time we got there. After seven long days in the saddle, with my body out of Long Riding shape and in pain from the winter off, we arrived in the stunning town of Grande Cache.

With the snowcapped Rocky Mountain cordillera on the horizon, I thanked Smokey and Mac for getting me this far by renting a corral for them at U Bar Ranch and buying extra hay from the owner. "Now we rest, kids," I said before giving each horse his grain.

IN THE FOOTHILLS of the Rocky Mountains, Grande Cache is a quaint town with a population of 3,500 people. An important outpost for the Hudson's Bay Company, the town got its name when fur trader Ignace Giasson cached a large supply of fur in the area during one of the winters between 1818 and 1821. The town is said to have been especially important for the company that helped build Canada.

Grande Cache is also home to Willmore Wilderness Park, a 4,600 square kilometer wilderness area next to the world-famous Jasper National Park. A beautiful place that doesn't have the marketing Jasper has but deserves to be visited. It's wild with breathtaking views. We rested the horses in the stunning town for a day. I wrote blogs and transferred the footage we had shot during the first week on the road to hard drives.

"We have been here since the '90s taking tourists into the mountains," Ray, the owner of U Bar Ranch, told me while we practiced social distancing. He was in his late fifties, with a thick mustache and an old worn-out straw hat on his head. His hands were either busy working or nestled in the deep pockets of his jean overalls.

Unfortunately, due to the previous summer's never-ending rain plus the pandemic keeping tourists away, he and his wife had decided to call it quits. "We figure this is as good a time to retire as ever," the cowboy who had competed in reining said with a half-smile on his pointy face.

It was sad to have to stay several feet away from Ray the whole time and feel like we shouldn't spend time around him. If we had arrived in Grande Cache the year before, I'm sure we would have eaten dinner with him and gotten to know this cowboy a lot better, like all the families who took us in before. However, with the current situation, sadly, that seemed like a relic of the distant past. We lived in a new world, a new reality, with new rules and regulations that seemed to change on the fly.

While I wrote blogs near Grande Cache Lake, Clara and I saw our first bear of the season. A teenage black bear grazed on the bright green grass near the motorhome while we watched it in wonder.

Clara studied the large beast. Petrified of bears, she said, "They're such beautiful animals. I just wish they weren't so dangerous. I don't know how you can ride out there by yourself for eight to ten hours every day. I wouldn't be able to do it."

"I just love seeing them from the comfort of the motorhome. Not so fun when I'm in the saddle," I told her.

It was near the lake that we also met a wonderful couple from Grande Prairie. From afar, they asked many questions about my journey and listened intently. They also loved to travel and explore the world. When we said goodbye, the wife put her arms around herself as if giving us a hug. When we went to drive off, we noticed there was a yellow plastic bag tied to the motorhome's right mirror. When I opened it, I found a bottle of Bodacious red wine, pizza bread, and a note.

The note read:

So awesome to meet and talk to you about your incredible journey. We would have loved to make you a home-cooked meal at our home, but we are in a hurry to get to our destination. Please accept this small token from us because, in our minds, you are bodacious, bold, adventurous, and so very humble and kind. Cheers as you finish the last leg of your amazing journey. Be safe and stay healthy.

Tom and Verna.

THIS PANDEMIC SURE changed the world and my journey in many ways, but it failed to erase the kindness in people's hearts!

22

THE ROAD TO HINTON

After a lovely day off in Grande Cache, it was time to get back on the road. On a sunny Friday morning, we started our ride toward the town of Hinton, 146 kilometers south. We continued over the foothills of the Rocky Mountains with the occasional glimpse of the cordillera's majesty. A lot of snow still covered the jagged peaks even though we were now in June.

On our third day out, we camped on a small road that ran to a large natural gas plant. While we tried to sleep, we could hear trucks honking on the nearby Highway 40. We wondered why every trucker that went by was slamming on the horn repeatedly.

"There must be a herd of caribou on the road," I told Clara.

All night, Smokey and Mac, who were tied to two trees, seemed more agitated than usual. They pawed the ground and stared off into the distance with their heads held high as if looking at some kind of danger.

The next morning, while we drank coffee and watched the boys eat their grain, a minivan stopped at the end of the short gravel road.

"Good morning!" a woman called. "I just saw your horses tied up and wanted to let you know there's a big sow grizzly with her cub just a few feet from here on the side of the highway!"

I could see the worry in her eyes. I thanked her and quickly began tacking up Mac to get out of there. The most dangerous situation you can be in with a grizzly is finding yourself near her cubs. The honking the previous night and the horses' nervousness all night now made sense. The momma bear must have been grazing near our camp. Thanks to the bell tied to Mac's neck ringing all night, the bear stayed away. This proved an ominous sign of what was yet to come.

Fearing the momma bear, I rode Mac south while Smokey followed in tow. Luckily, we did not see the bear and she didn't see us. Everything was going well until about six kilometers later, when out of the forest, a huge male grizzly stepped into view, out of the woods and into the ditch. Mac immediately saw him and turned around, ready to run the other way. Smokey didn't see the bear, but Mac's reaction was enough to turn him around as well and try to take off with his adoptive brother.

"Easy, boys! Easy!" I cried out, using all my might to hold both horses from taking off at a gallop back the way we had come.

In my head, I could hear Mac saying back to me, "Did you see the size of that thing?"

With the tall buckskin standing on his hind legs, fighting me, the bear turned around and wandered back into the bush.

I sighed with relief and managed to turn the boys around. They stood with their heads held high, pushing a tad higher every few seconds, ears pointed forward and nostrils open wide. Smokey snorted repeatedly. After about five minutes, man and beasts finally calmed down. With no sign of the grizzly, we continued south on the other side of the road.

After that, anything — and I mean anything — set the boys off. A large rock, a fallen tree, a weird-looking hill. To them, everything was that bear, and it was out to eat them. This was the only bear we actually saw, although we did ride by many piles of scat and fresh holes dug by grizzlies searching for roots.

On this stretch, we managed to raise $170 for the Barretos Children's Cancer Hospital. A trucker who worked with Gregg —the guy who pulled the motorhome out of the mud — and a fellow who worked for the Caribou Watch Program made donations on the side of the road.

"What you are doing is awesome! Happy to help in some small way," Mr. Ferrera said after parking his truck and passing me a $100 bill.

Before he left, like everyone else I spoke to, he warned me of the bears. "Just please be very careful in this area with the grizzlies. They're big and mean," he offered, before jumping back to the safety of his truck and leaving me in the dust.

"Big and mean, you say," I whispered.

AFTER FIVE LONG days on the road, we arrived at Old Entrance, but not before riding by a foul-smelling dead and headless moose. Not a pretty sight. The smell, a mixture of rotting garbage and wet dog, nearly made me puke. But what a view we were awarded during the final kilometers of the day! Right in front of Smokey's ears sat the Rocky Mountains. They looked more beautiful than ever, glowing in the afternoon sun. Only seventy kilometers east of Jasper National Park, we were in one of the most stunning places on Earth. God's country.

I took in the view and gave thanks. Thanks to my powerful horses. Thanks to Aaron Stelkia and Jim McCrae for entrusting me with these animals. Thanks to my selfless girlfriend, Clara. Thanks to Rocky and Marie Aitken for lending us the support vehicle. Thanks to Sara Turner. Thanks to all the kind souls who helped us during this final journey. Thanks to the Universe for awarding me this view and this blessed life.

Just after 2 p.m., we arrived at Old Entrance, an old train station turned horsey bed and breakfast. Situated next to the Athabasca River, the stunning property looked like Horse Heaven.

Neatly trimmed green grass and bright yellow dandelions danced on the banks of the wide, fast-moving Athabasca River as a herd of seven horses of all colors and sizes happily grazed. There were several black and white pintos, big and strong like a Percheron, and some other smaller animals. A very nice-looking herd, unbothered by my presence.

When I made it to her house, Mary, the owner of the B&B, practiced social distancing. From afar, she said, "Welcome to Old Entrance!"

Clara and I continued to stay as far away from people as possible. Due to the pandemic, we were traveling down small roads, high lining the horses every night. When we arrived in a town like this one, we looked for a place to rent a corral and a place to park the motorhome.

Before, I would have asked a local rancher or farmer for help, eaten dinner with them, and helped them work on a fence line. I'd hug the children before leaving as if I'd become a part of the family. That was all in the past. In this new world, renting a corral seemed like the safest option, so I turned Mac and Smokey out in their corral before thanking them for their hard work.

After only thirteen days, we were already 322 kilometers south of Grande Prairie and 2,922 kilometers south of Fairbanks, Alaska, our starting point for this Last Long Ride!

Feeding the boys, I sat in their corral watching them eat. Smokey chased Mac away from the hay pile he chose to eat from every couple of minutes. Putting his ears straight back, and like a shark, he lunged at Mac, showing his teeth. Although he was the smaller horse, standing at 14.3 hands on his tippy toes, he was by far the leader of the herd.

Mac, a 17 hand gentle giant, had what Clara and I called "small horse syndrome." We were convinced that, in his mind, he believed he was a tiny pony. The big buckskin would allow Smokey to boss him around all day and was scared of basically anything and everything. He also did not like to lead while we rode south. Mac would much rather play the safe role of carrying the pack and hiding behind Smokey all day.

Other than their funny and sometimes annoying quirks, they were amazing animals. When I first started working with Smokey, he didn't know how to stop, walk in a straight line, or stand still while I got on. I could only ride him in the round pen and even that meant get on and hold on.

During this journey, Mac and Smokey became seasoned long-distance travelers. Both crossed bridges, cities and towns, mountains, rivers, and more. It was amazing to see them mature under me. I couldn't have been prouder of my kids. These two powerful beasts allowed me to travel double the kilometers I used to ride in a month with my other horses. Their strength was unbelievable.

Before leaving the corral, I said, "I love you boys."

DURING OUR LAYOVER in Old Entrance, I was finally allowed to tell the world the secret I had been holding for the past year.

The previous July, Dana Peers, the president of the Calgary Stampede, had invited me to lead the 2020 parade. When he asked me to become the Calgary Stampede Parade Marshal I felt like I was in a dream. And quite honestly, I never saw that career high point coming.

After the invitation, Dana told me I would have to keep the news a secret until 2020. I am the worst person in the world when it comes to secrets. However, after signing a non-disclosure contract, I obviously got better. I didn't want to blow it. The marshal leads the parade that opens the rodeo and is an ambassador for the Stampede. In a normal year, the marshal would give speeches at special events and participate in the rodeo's grand entry.

A few months earlier, before driving to Alaska to begin my Last Long Ride, I met Dana in Calgary. I asked if he would allow me to finish my ride in the 2020 Calgary Stampede rodeo. I made him laugh with my humble request. "I just need you guys to leave the gate open."

Dana had this laugh that started deep in his gut and built its way up and out. His laughter made everyone around him laugh as well. It was contagious. He promised to allow me into the Stampede Park at the end of my journey and to ride with me during my final leg. He is a true cowboy who loves Western culture!

When I gave him a signed copy of my first book, *Long Ride Home*, and included in the dedication an invitation to ride with me, I never imagined he would take me up on it. Nor that he would award me one of the biggest honors of my life on the same day.

Flash forward to April of 2020 when we were set to make the big announcement in front of the Canadian media. I would finally get to tell the world my colossal secret. Due to the COVID-19 pandemic, the unveiling was canceled along with the Stampede. I wanted to cry. However, everyone in the world had their plans canceled in 2020. There was no time to feel sorry for myself.

While working with the horses in Osoyoos, awaiting COVID-19 restrictions to lift in the province of Alberta, Dana called me one afternoon and said he was still going to announce the 2020 parade marshal, even with no parade to lead. "Your story needs to be shared," Dana told me. "The world needs this message, now more than ever."

I felt blessed. Honored. Relieved. We set the big day for Tuesday, June 2.

By June 1, my heart could hardly contain my excitement. The following morning, we would announce live on national television that I was this year's marshal. I had interviews booked with Global News, CTV, Citytv, CBC, CBC French, and Canadian radio stations and television stations in Brazil. Since the interviews started at 6 a.m., I went to bed early.

Clara startled me awake at midnight. "Your phone is ringing!"

My only thought was that someone had died. It was Jason Coxford, director of corporate communications at the Stampede. I was so dazed, I had no idea what to expect. "Filipe, I know you are probably sleeping already. I'm so sorry, but we can't make the announcement tomorrow," Coxford said in a low voice.

I sat in silence. The reason for yet another postponement of the announcement was the Blackout Tuesday movement. It was started by the music industry to raise awareness about police brutality and systemic racism. It was set off by the death of George Floyd, a forty-six-year-old black man who was pinned to the ground and suffocated on May 25, 2020, by a Minneapolis police officer. The officer was charged with murder for his actions. As a result, people were urged to use Tuesday, June 2, as a day to reflect on racism by not posting anything on social media.

I'd studied journalism in university and started Journey America in part to show others that we are all inherently the same regardless of our religion, nationality, or skin color. I hoped to inspire a more just world. As a supporter of the Black Lives Matter movement, I completely agreed with Coxford.

My secret would have to wait one more day. As frustrating as it was, it was for a good reason.

23

500 KILOMETERS TO CALGARY

-

Finally, on a sunny June 3, the world learned that I was the 2020 Calgary Stampede Parade Marshal.

My day began with a 5 a.m. interview for CBC Radio Calgary. It started well, but at one point the host threw me a curveball. "Filipe, how do you feel traveling with your horses while the rest of Canada sits at home in lockdown due to this pandemic?"

This was my biggest fear. I took a deep breath and answered as well as I could, "We waited for the province of Alberta to take down its restrictions and open the provincial and national parks in the province. My girlfriend and I changed our route to stay away from people and are self-sufficient with our support vehicle."

Luckily, this was the only time anyone had anything negative to say about the final leg of my journey. All the other television hosts and journalists were super kind to me and celebrated what I had done. Everyone was excited to hear a positive story amid so many months of suffering and negativity!

It was a long day. I cried, I laughed, I told stories from my odyssey until late in the afternoon. It was such an emotional rollercoaster that at night, I barely had enough energy to eat and was left with no voice. It was so worth it, though!

The following morning, I was in every major newspaper and on television shows and radio stations in Canada. My story had also made a resurgence in the Brazilian media where I was already well known. For an author, these opportunities are extremely important because it's immensely helpful in selling books.

BEFORE WE RODE out of Old Entrance, we were visited by Rocky and Marie Aitken, and as always, they came bearing gifts! When they arrived at the horsey B&B, Marie announced, "I brought banana bread for you guys and hay for the horses."

It was so nice seeing them and getting to spend a few days by their side. While Clara and I barbecued over charcoal, I told Rocky and Marie, "Today you two will eat as we do in Brazil and Argentina." It was a wonderful night.

The following day, while Mac and Smokey rested, Marie and Rocky drove us south to see the route we would be trekking down in a few days. Before we got on the gravel Forestry Trunk Road 734, the old Highway 40, Rocky warned, "If it rains a lot, you guys might not get through with the motorhome."

My original plan was to ride down the Cowboy Trail toward Calgary. Dotted with ranches and people, it was the perfect antidote for the solitude that had marked much of the journey. It felt just right for me to travel down the Cowboy Trail to the Calgary Stampede to end this very Long Ride. Sadly, that plan was thrown out the window due to the ongoing health crisis. Even though this gravel road wasn't in the best shape, we made the decision to follow it south.

On a gray Wednesday morning, I rode out of Old Entrance and started my ride down the old Highway 40 to my final destination. The Forestry Trunk Road offered gorgeous views of the mountains and the lack of traffic was a welcome break. On average, about ten to fifteen cars drove by each day. On the weekends, things got a little crazy as Calgarians drove up to camp, but it was still better than following a highway.

Because the gravel road ran through Crown land, campers didn't have to pay anything to spend a night or seven. There were makeshift camping spots next to the road the entire way south. This meant there was no shortage of places to call home for the night. They offered shade for the horses, tons of grass for grazing, and, most of the time, water. It was Long Riding heaven! The most important part was that we didn't have to enter people's homes and risk spreading the virus.

"We could stay here for a month," Clara said as we camped one night in a gorgeous spot overlooking the Rocky Mountains. Watching the horses graze on tall grass with their hobbles and a small stream running next to them, I agreed.

On our sixth day on the Forestry Trunk Road, Dana Peers and his wife Laura came to spend the day with us. "I've been looking forward to this for weeks," Dana said while we tacked up the horses in the early morning.

We spent an amazing day riding through the foothills together while Clara and Laura drove ahead and found a place for lunch. With Dana atop Mac and me on Smokey, we discussed politics, the economy, the global pandemic, and life. I loved every second of it.

"I hope you're hungry," Laura said when we finally stopped for our lunch break. She wasn't joking! The Italian-Canadian hairdresser brought enough food for a soccer team.

"Laura, now I know you really are Italian," I joked as she kept pulling out Tupperware containers from a large blue cooler. Laura was a thin, petite blond with a massive heart. She was soft-spoken like Dana, and they adopted us from that point on. Clara and I fell in love with them immediately. Their energy, humor, and light take on life was a lot like ours.

While we sat around chatting and drinking beers after lunch, Dana said, "When our son Dusty passed away, we realized what's really important in this life. It's moments like this."

Sadly, in July of 2012, as I began the journey of my life, Dusty's life ended in a terrible car accident. He was only eighteen. Dana, Laura, and their older son Cody loved Dusty dearly. I can't even imagine how hard life became for them after he passed.

"There's not a second that goes by when I don't think of him," Laura told us as she looked off into the distance, her eyes filling with tears, her hands pressed together tightly.

Dusty was an amazing person and artist, and Dana and Laura have started different scholarships to celebrate his life. One of those initiatives is centered around the Calgary Stampede poster. In past years, the organization would contract an established artist to draw the artwork, an iconic part of the legendary rodeo. But in 2019, Dana started the Calgary Stampede Poster Competition, one of the largest art scholarships in Canada with $20,000 distributed among the top eight finalists.

"We joined forces with the Flock family, who also lost their child at an early age, in order to make this happen," Dana explained. This is an amazing opportunity for youth to showcase their talent on a world stage. It's also a way to allow Dusty's memory to live forever through these talented youth and their creations. This was just one of many scholarships the couple founded. "At the end of the day, I just love seeing what these kids are able to accomplish, and it brings Laura and me a lot of joy," Dana said.

While we talked, the horses munched on green grass in a corral nearby. We rarely found corrals on this journey, especially ones with knee-high pasture. Clara and I agreed this was the best day ever! At one point, a woman came up to ask if we were going to spend the night there.

"We had found this spot first, and when we returned to set up camp, you guys were here," she said, a little nervous. I made her feel better when I told her we were only having lunch and would soon ride out. She flashed me a smile and thanked me.

A little later, she came back and asked if she could take a photo of the horses. I said of course, and while she snapped photos of Smokey lying down and twitching every couple of seconds from dreams or nightmares, I asked her what she was up to. By now, two trucks were parked near us, and several people ran around, almost in a military manner. They were unloading ATVs from a trailer and gathering equipment as if they were on an important mission.

"We are here looking for Bigfoot. There have been many sightings in this area," she said with a straight face.

I was so in shock, in awe of what this woman had just told me, I had no reaction. I simply stared at her with a frozen look on my face.

"You think we're crazy, don't you?" she asked after a few seconds of silence.

"No, not at all! I just wasn't expecting that answer," I said, trying to defuse the awkward situation.

She went back to her friends, and I told Dana, Laura, and Clara about their search for Bigfoot. Everyone had the same frozen expression I had mustered up only minutes earlier.

"If they're looking for Bigfoot, why are they doing it on noisy ATVs? Shouldn't they be sneaking around the forest quietly?" Clara protested as they started up their loud machines. The horses, now at the edge of the corral, worried about the combusting engines.

"I bet they think I'm the crazy one riding horses across continents," I said. "To each their own!"

Everyone laughed.

After eating way too much veal, salad, fruit, and crackers, we continued our ride south. By early afternoon we arrived at Chungo Creek Outfitters, our home for two nights.

Dana and I untacked the horses in front of a log tack room and gave them their feed. After organizing everything, Dana went over the plan for my arrival in Calgary in a few weeks. The organization had to apply for special permission to have a procession, not a parade, to safely escort me to Stampede Park.

"To prevent people from congregating, we had to assure the city we would not release our route ahead of time," Dana said while we looked over the plan and the streets we would be traveling through. He had printed out the map of the entire route. The thought of entering a city with 1.3 million residents with two wild horses made me swallow with a dry mouth. After crossing metal-grate bridges, the Yukon, encountering herds of bison, and dealing with bears, this would be our final test. Maybe it would be the most dangerous of them all. But there was no turning back now! We were only 350 kilometers away from the end having ridden more than 25,000 kilometers.

Let that sink in.

24

FOR ELLEN CRISTINA

At Chungo Creek Outfitters, we traveled to another world, one where, for a second, COVID-19 didn't seem to exist. "You need anything, just let me know," the owner said.

Corey Kristoff was a man built like a WWE wrestler. His smile was that of a veteran hockey player. He was missing one of his top teeth due to a horse that had pawed him in the face a few years before. "I had tied this horse to the back of the truck and was leading him slowly back to camp, but he kept stepping over the lead rope. One of the times I went to help him get his front leg free, the bastard struck me in the face." He recalled how he was forced to go straight to the dentist to have surgery.

"I was back on the mountain that night," he concluded. His son didn't let him get the hole in his mouth fixed. "He says the toothless smile is a part of me now."

Chungo Creek Outfitters had operated in the Nordegg, Alberta area for over seventeen years. In addition to horseback adventures, they also provided various guiding services like jet boat tours, fishing trips, and drop camps. They rented out rustic cabins year-round.

While we watched Mac and Smokey munch hay, Corey told me in a low raspy voice, "My dad used to farm in southern Alberta. One day, he saw an ad for this place at a diner. The next thing we knew, he sold the farm, and we were learning how to guide pack trips into the mountains."

The first night we were there, alongside Corey's mom and dad and several friends from Alberta, we enjoyed a delicious BBQ. With COVID-19 restrictions being lifted in Canada, this was the first outdoor gathering we had been to in a long time. It felt weird being around the ten people present, but it also felt like things were finally going back to normal, slowly but surely.

Over succulent chicken and fresh salad, Corey talked about the adventures he had lived in this gorgeous part of the world. From thunderstorms to raging rivers to grizzlies to freezing temperatures, out in these mountains there's never an easy day or a dull moment. But like me, Corey wouldn't change his life for anything in this world.

"I love it, you know. The freedom to be out in those mountains with my horses, doing what I love, immersed in nature, it's priceless," Corey told me while taking a long swig of Coors.

I agreed with him!

The next day, Corey's father Greg took us for a ride in his side by side deep into a stunning valley. We marveled at the view while we tried to stay dry and warm. A terrible rain left us soaked.

"Sorry, I forgot there was no roof in the back," the elderly gentleman said as we laughed.

Greg told us some of the wildest stories I have ever heard in my life! Like the time a big male grizzly nearly ate a child who had fallen from his steed, right in front of him, only to be saved by his son Corey.

"The kid had wide eyes for weeks," Greg said remembering the close call, laughing so hard he nearly choked. There were also stories of tragedies, like the time they lost an entire string of horses crossing a raging river.

"The horses were all tied together. We were still learning how to be outfitters," he said, shaking his head. The mountains offered a steep learning curve that was unforgiving. Out there, the line between fun and tragedy, life and death, was very thin. I had learned that lesson once or twice, too!

Inside the intricate log cabin that Cory built with the help of a team of horses and his brother, we ate breakfast and lunch every day. We even got to celebrate Greg's birthday while we were there. It was the greatest stopover ever! "Happy birthday, sir," I told Greg. I felt as if I had known the big Albertan my entire life.

From Chungo Creek Outfitters, we began our final 330-kilometer trek to Calgary. It felt extraordinary to be so close to the finish line, especially since everyone was so healthy and well. Clara and I had managed to stay safe and healthy and Mac and Smokey were fat, exuding energy. More importantly, their feet and backs — two of the hardest things to keep healthy on a long ride — were perfect. I was so happy.

"You boys look so good for your big procession into Calgary!" I said to my kids. We followed the Forestry Trunk Road across Highway 11. Before the day was over, I rode by a sign that gave me the chills. The green sign on the right side of the picturesque gravel road read: Calgary 306 kilometers.

I wanted to scream with happiness! By then, I had dreamt of seeing a sign with the word Calgary on it for years. And here we were, right in front of it. We were closer than ever to reaching our goal. It felt surreal to be nearing the end of my Last Long Ride!

However, like many times before on these journeys, what happened next took me from the heavens straight to the depths of hell. Shortly after taking photos in front of the sign, we found a nice place to camp for the night. After untacking the boys and feeding them some grain, I put on their hobbles and let them graze on the tall, bright green grass.

Clara and I munched on our dinner while I watched the boys hop from here to there, grazing contentedly. Little blackbirds sat on their backs, happily going for a ride. All of a sudden, Smokey laid down hard on the ground and stuck his head straight forward on the grass with both ears back flat. A house sparrow and a common grackle stood on his back and mane.

"Oh, no! This is bad," is all I managed to get out to Clara before I ran to him and got him up. Smokey was showing early signs of colic.

"What do we do?" Clara asked with tears filling her eyes, panic taking over.

My voice cracked. "We don't allow him to lay down again or roll, and we walk him around!"

I poured a large amount of cooking oil down his throat in the hope it would lubricate his long intestine and hopefully cause him to defecate.

As we walked the mighty gray horse around the open field, I tried to rid myself of the negative thoughts that plagued my mind: *You are going to lose him. It's always at the end that tragedy strikes. Smokey is going to die!*

At that moment, I was transported to the final days of my Long Ride to the End of the World. Specifically, to the heart of Tierra Del Fuego, Touhlin, where a piece of my heart died along with my son Sapito Gonzales. That was the worst day of my life!

After the friendly rancher who was hosting us gave my criollo alfalfa cubes, he had terrible colic caused by a severe intoxication. After fighting for an entire night, he took his last breath, his big golden head in my lap.

The local vet had several possible theories for Sapito's sudden death. The horse had ridden into the small town as healthy as a race-horse only twenty-four hours earlier! Something was wrong with the alfalfa cubes the rancher fed him. "Either a rat urinated inside the bag, or some of the cubes had gone moldy, or they came bad from the factory. This was intoxication from those cubes," the elderly vet concluded.

I would never know the truth, only conjecture. It could have been any number of things. Poison even crossed my mind. The only thing I knew for sure was anger and the pain of his loss. Only 100 kilometers from the end of our arduous journey, having already ridden more than 7,000 kilometers, and to the literal end of the world, my beloved Sapito was gone. I blamed myself.

Now, here I was again in the same situation, so close to the end of another Long Ride and with a horse in a life-or-death situation. I desperately tried to wipe the frozen images of suffering from Touhlin out of my mind. It wasn't easy. The worst part was that I didn't have any medication on me. Canada had recently instituted a law where only a certified veterinarian could administer drugs to treat an animal. None could sell me anything to take on the journey in case of an emergency like this one.

I tried to buy at least Benamine, a muscle relaxant, from several Canadian vets, but I had no luck. "I'm sorry, but it's illegal," one vet said, making me feel like I was trying to do something wrong.

With no other options, we kept walking Smokey. I contacted the closest vet at a clinic in Rocky Mountain House, some ninety kilometers away. If Smokey kept getting worse, the vet said he would come to see him, but at a cost of $500, and that was just to drive out. Medication and treatment would be extra.

While we walked the wild horse around, he tightened up with abdominal pains every few minutes. It was painful to watch. His sides would contract, vibrating, making him let out a loud grunt while putting his muzzle towards his flank, ears back flat.

"It's okay, buddy, you're going to be okay," I told him, cringing with the pain he was feeling.

Clara drove back to Chungo Creek Outfitters where Corey lent us some Phenylbutazone (Bute), a white powder that acts as an analgesic (pain reliever) and anti-inflammatory medication for horses. It wasn't Benamine, but at least it would give him some relief from the pain, and it was all Corey had.

I continued to walk him around. He tried to lie down often, stopping once every five minutes and shaking with pain. Finally, after several tense hours, Smokey first defecated and a couple of minutes later, coughed out a thick green slime. He snorted some more of the liquid out of his nose and fell asleep standing up. That's when I started breathing a little easier.

"That's it, buddy! Relax," I said to my mighty pony. Then, after a five-minute snooze, he awoke, put his head down, and started grazing.

"Yes!" I yelled in happiness! We had done it. Smokey was going to be okay. *We* were going to be okay!

THE MORNING after Smokey gave us the scare of our lives, he awoke as if nothing had ever happened. When he saw me, he whinnied with excitement like he did every morning before I gave him his grain.

"Sorry, buddy! No feed for you this morning," I told the gray. He loved feed so much, some days he would rear and whinny at the same time like a movie horse! Due to the colic, I decided to cut his feed for a couple of days just to be safe. He was alert, happy, hungry, and showed no sign of pain. I thought about letting the boys rest that day, but finally concluded that walking would do Smokey the most good. I saddled Mac, ponied Smokey, and headed south.

That morning, a few minutes into our day, I received a terribly sad message from Brazil. Ellen Cristina, the young teen who had named her teddy-bunny after me, had taken her last breath. Her cancer unfortunately won the fight. She finally rested.

I said a long prayer for Ellen from the saddle and offered my ride to her. "Thank you for giving me the opportunity to meet another angel," I said, gazing at the dark clouds above. Almost as soon as I said amen, the heavy rain that would accompany us for days began to fall. It was as if the Universe was in mourning.

That afternoon, while we rested the horses on the side of a gravel road, I realized I'd lost one of the GoPro cameras the night before.

"It must have fallen out of my jacket pocket while I walked Smokey around last night," I told Clara.

She drove back to our previous camp to search for the small camera. Clara returned two hours later empty-handed. "I searched everywhere...nothing," she said, disappointed.

We had a second GoPro, but the card that was inside the lost camera contained a lot of footage from the past few days. It was a sad loss.

After two more rainy days on the road, we rode into Ram River

Falls Campground. A herd of about thirty scraggly-looking mountain goats watched us curiously. I untacked the boys and offered them water, but their wide eyes were on the mountain goats as if they were devils.

"They look homeless, but they're nice," I told Smokey and Mac, assuring them they were fine.

The next day, Clara and the boys rested at the campground while I drove back to Nordegg to do live interviews with press in Canada and Brazil and teach my monthly class for Brazilian school kids via Cisco's WebEx teleconference tool. It was an initiative I started with my good friend Marcos Silva in Brazil and his technology company Added. We raised funds together to donate a computer, projector, screen, and one year of high-speed internet to a public school in Junqueiropolis in the interior of São Paulo. Along with thirty smartphones!

I rode a horse to the school, making the kids go crazy, and gave my motivational talk. We gave each student a copy of my first book. The teachers were using the manuscript to teach Portuguese, writing, grammar, geography, biology, and to discuss and plan their life projects, goals, and dreams for the future.

During my ride from Alaska to Calgary, I connected with the kids once a month to teach them about a different subject relating to my ride and about how to plan their own projects. That week, we discussed Canada's national parks, recycling, and sustainability.

Clara was able to stay with the horses while I drove the sixty kilometers there and back as I searched for an internet signal. You know the saying, "There's no rest for the wicked"? Well, out there on the road, rest is reserved for my horses and my horses only. I just couldn't find enough hours in the day to do everything I needed to do.

When I finally arrived back at the campground late that afternoon, Clara told me, happy as ever, "Some nice lady gave me a delicious slice of apple pie."

Mac and Smokey grazed nearby. This was the first time on the journey that I left her to tend Smokey and Mac on her own. "I was so nervous on the way back wondering if everyone was okay," I said, giving my gorgeous girlfriend a hug.

With her in my arms, the butterflies in my stomach began to flap their wings. With the end of this journey so close to the end, I was about to make the most important decision of my existence. The thought of actually asking my *flor del pago* to spend the rest of my life with me was really scary, but I had never been so sure of anything in my life. That might be what scared me most!

As I neared the end of this epic chapter in my story, I also neared the beginning of another journey, one that would start on one knee with a ring, a promise, and a kiss. But first, I had to cross the finish line and escape yet another brush with an old sharp-toothed friend.

25

THE LAST DANCE

On a beautiful Saturday, July 20, Clara and I went to visit Ram River Falls. Without a single cloud in the deep blue sky, we were in awe of the fall's magnitude and beauty.

As we took in the beauty of the thick white veil of water falling into the river below, I said to Clara, "I thought it was going to be something way smaller."

In the background, we could see several rams hanging out on a very steep ridge that stood higher than the falls. Their footing was extraordinary! Deep in the dark gray and black canyon where the cascade hit the river below, a bright rainbow appeared in the mist.

"This is stunning," Clara said before we climbed the steep metal staircase back to the horses. We ate a light breakfast that morning before I began riding south. This was the last dance.

After crossing an antique, bright-orange metal-framed bridge with a wooden deck, seven propeller airplanes flew over the horses super low. The noise from the flying devils scared the boys into a gallop, and I had to do some convincing to get them to stop and relax.

They have to have one last freak-out before Calgary, I thought. With the gravel road to myself and no cars in sight, I simply laughed. "I thought you liked airplanes, Mac?"

After only two hours in the saddle, I was surprised by Marie Aitken and her niece Jayce who hauled horses up to ride with us. "I told you I was going to ride with you on this journey," Marie said.

We unloaded their big, beautiful Quarter Horses. It was so nice having people to ride with! We laughed, shared stories, and took in the natural beauty around us. It had been years since Marie last jumped into the saddle, more than two decades! And here she was, looking proud atop a beautiful palomino gelding. Her father was a successful rancher and talented horseman, so Marie grew up around these animals. It must have felt good to be atop a Quarter Horse again!

When it came time to call it a day, we miraculously found a corral in the middle of nowhere. "This is the cherry on our cake of a day," I told Marie and Jayce in excitement.

Our recent visitors were bringing us luck. With a herd of cows and their cute calves staring at us with curiosity, we untacked the horses and cooked a delicious BBQ lunch. It was a tad ironic.

After Marie and Jayce bid us farewell, it was time to welcome another visitor to camp! Ted Stovin and his girlfriend, Storm Dafoe, came to interview us for their podcast "Cowboy Sh*t."

"You said you liked beer so I brought a cooler full," Ted told me as he opened the white lid, making me levitate with happiness.

I wanted to kiss him. The cooler was packed with cans and bottles from different breweries. "You're welcome out any time you want, brother, as long as you come with this cooler!"

Ted laughed. We drank the cold beers, talked about cowboy shit, and recorded an amazing podcast that night.

THE FINAL 160 kilometers of my Last Long Ride were nothing short of an epic adventure! It started with a visit from a male grizzly bear that decided to follow us. He was big, beautiful, and petrifying. After encountering bears nearly every day since we departed from Fairbanks, sometimes three in a day, the horses and I kept our cool.

"There's a herd of wild horses ahead," Clara announced while setting up the tripod in front of the motorhome to get a shot.

I excitedly scanned the horizon for the herd. I searched and searched with no luck until finally I spotted a low, dark shape walking out of the forest toward the road.

A colt, I thought to myself.

As I watched the dark figure's head pop up onto the road, I realized that was no colt. What gave it away was the protruding hump on its furry back, and the odd way it walked, like a human hunched over on its hands and feet.

"Shit, it's a grizzly," I whispered.

My horses were already looking straight at the bear, heads held high and raising just a tad higher every couple of seconds. With my legs, I could feel Smokey's pulse race.

The bear was about five meters in front of us, to our right side. When he saw us, he stopped in his tracks and smelled the cool air.

My horses also stood their ground, looking straight at him. Although my heart raced in my chest, the same beat per minute as Smokey's, I kept calm, and so did my horses. It was a beautiful moment I will never forget. Exhilarating.

The grizzly was so majestic and so close to us that I could take in all his beauty: his strong face, short, rounded ears, large shoulder hump, his long sharp teeth and claws, and his powerful stocky legs. I was mesmerized. After what seemed like an eternity, he continued across the road slowly without taking his gaze off us. The horses did the same to him.

When he got to the other side of the road, he made his way to the tree line and began walking in our direction. Unsure of what to do, I kicked the horses up to the other side of the road, walking forward. When the horses crossed the imaginary line where the bear was now behind them, still on the other side of the road, they both tried to run off. I held onto them, and they continued on, prancing slowly until they settled back into a walk.

Looking back, I saw him come out of the tree line and onto the road. With his nose pointed towards my horses, he followed us for a while, again smelling the cool air and shaking his head from side to side. It was one of the coolest moments of my life, magical, as if that bear was telling me I had passed my test. I had become one with nature. He wasn't afraid of us nor was I scared of him. We both respected one another and simply wanted to get a closer look. After being so afraid of these larger-than-life beasts, extremely nervous and fearful with every encounter, this final meeting couldn't have gone better.

And to top it off, since Clara thought there were wild horses ahead, she filmed the entire encounter. When we met up minutes later up the road, she was ecstatic. "I think I just got the best shot of the entire trip!"

Half an hour after our meeting with the bear, the horses and I crossed Corkscrew Mountain through a hairy pass that hugged a jagged mountain face. On the other side was a thousand-foot drop to a shallow river below, with no guardrail to separate the gravel road from the abyss, it made for a harrowing ride. Mac and Smokey handled it all with bravery and class. I'm so proud of these two wild horses.

At Barrier Mountain Outfitters, we left the horses to rest and drove to Sundre, Alberta for a much-needed shower. It had been seven days since our last. Then we went on to interviews with CBC, Global Television, and Globo in Brazil. Finally, we picked up a special friend.

"Looking good, cowboy," Shelagh Haney said outside of Tim Hortons, guitar case in hand.

"I can't believe you actually came back," I said after we embraced. With Shelagh around, Clara and I were able to ride together for the final week of this epic journey, something we had been dreaming about for a long time!

"This makes me so happy," said Clara one afternoon as we neared the end of the day. She proudly sat atop her baby, Smokey.

It was so nice having Shelagh with us. Her energy, humor, angelic singing voice, and intelligence were a breath of fresh air.

She also rode with me for a few hours every day. One morning, she nearly died. I saw everything happen in slow motion. Riding Smokey on a windy day, my childhood friend lost her baseball cap. I got off Mac and handed it to her. To prevent it from flying off her head again, she decided to hang it on the saddle horn. We continued south, chatting with a few cowboys and cowgirls from the area who were riding with us for the day.

Suddenly, out of the corner of my eye, I first saw Shelagh's hat fall from the saddle. Smokey took off like a bullet straight for the highway. It all happened so quickly, I didn't have time to react. A pickup truck hauling a large trailer was flying north. Shelagh and Smokey were headed straight towards the truck. I prepared to see the worst scene of my life.

In a last-minute effort, Shelagh managed to turn Smokey back onto the shoulder, and the Universe granted her a longer life.

"Oh, my dear God," I said, taking the first breath in what felt like years. Luckily, Shelagh grew up riding in Caledon East, Ontario and managed to stay on and turn Smokey away from the road. What a scare so close to the end!

"That was close," Shelagh admitted when she finally managed to calm Smokey down and we regrouped. Wide-eyed and shaking, I passed her the hat.

"Put this thing on your head and tighten it up," I told her.

"Aye, Captain," she replied.

That afternoon, Spencer Hazelwood, my childhood friend and high school roping partner, who now lives in Alberta, found a place for Mac and Smokey to rest. Not only that, he hosted us for dinner at his friend Phillip Schellenberg's house.

"So nice seeing you, bud!" Spencer told me.

Our new friend Phillip was a real cowboy who ran a big ranch with his family just north of Cochrane in the Morley and Water Valley. He wore a black felt cowboy hat, had a light blue rag tied around his neck, and walked with a slight limp. Like all true cowboys, he was either healing from an injury or permanently injured from a wreck. "I saw you guys camping just down the road a few days ago and thought about coming out to see if you needed anything." We couldn't believe the coincidence.

We shared beers and two party-sized pizzas. Seventeen large white wolf pelts hung in Phillip's shop. He was a master trapper. When I spotted the pelts, I immediately looked at Shelagh to see her reaction. With her mom's work saving animals, I knew it was a huge contradiction for her to be in this shop with seventeen huge and stunning dead wolves.

To me, she mouthed, "Mother would have a heart attack." However, she listened to Philip's family, heard their stories, and learned about their way of life without judging. Shelagh and her mom were both extraordinary environmentalists. Her mom did important work to preserve several species, but they weren't extremists. There was dialogue, empathy, and understanding. I really loved them for this.

As we got to know Philip's family, we learned that his older daughter became the first girl to qualify at the Canadian Finals Rodeo for the junior steer riding event. Bailey, a teenager with a wicked smile, was only fifteen years old at the time.

For her mom, Naomi Schellenberg, it was not so cool, especially since Bailey suffered a concussion. However, Bailey said she is addicted to the feeling she gets when she climbs on the back of a thousand-pound steer.

After our pizza party, Phillip, Spencer, and I had a tie-down roping competition on an electric roping dummy the family owned. When you sat on the metal horse, you could squeeze your legs to release a calf dummy that would slide away from the horse on little wheels. Obviously, Phillip roped the fastest and won!

My ego was bruised by the cowboy with the English version of my name. He had more skill with the old lariat. "Rematch!" I yelled. We all laughed.

The following morning was a terrible, rainy day. Phillip's two daughters saddled their horses at 6 a.m. and rode out to meet me. They were drenched, so they made a pit stop at a friend's house first to put their clothes in the dryer. Then they continued to the corrals where Mac and Smokey were resting.

"I can't believe you girls rode for three hours in the rain just to get here and ride with me today," I said to the two blonde cowgirls. Soaked from the cold rain, but radiating warm smiles, they sat on their steeds proudly. It was an amazing day in the saddle with the girls and some more teens from nearby ranches.

While we rode, Bailey told me about a mountain lion she shot a few months before that was now at the taxidermist. "It's a big, beautiful cat. When I get my driver's license, I'm going to sell it and buy a car."

THE NIGHT before our arrival at the Calgary Stampede, I made a friend for life. "It's a pleasure meeting you, sir," said Kynan Vine, the manager of western events at the Greatest Outdoor Show on Earth. The retired bullfighter, known as Cowboy Kynan by his fellow staff, couldn't get over the fact that I would arrive at the stampede grounds on the exact day I said I would. I'd made my prediction over a year earlier!

"When they first told me about you riding in the parade, coming from Alaska on horseback, I told them there's no way, man. There's no way he will arrive on time, man!"

Kynan was in his early thirties, of medium build, and had thin light blond hair and a chiseled jawline fit for a Ken doll that made him look a lot like my friend Tuf Cooper. "I get that all the time," he told me when I called out the similarity with the World Champion tie-down roper.

It wasn't just Kynan's love for rodeo and Western culture that made us seem like old friends right away. He also loved Brazil and its culture and had even visited my country.

"My wife Megan lived in Brazil as an exchange student when she was in high school. We went down a few years ago to see the family who hosted her," he told me before cooking us traditional *pão de queijo* (cheese bread) and succulent meat.

"Am I in Brazil right now?" I asked, digging into the delicious dinner while he showed me photos of his time in South America's largest country.

While Clara, Shelagh, and I took turns showering in his basement, Kynan told us why he had to retire early from bullfighting. "In 2013, my mom got sick and needed a kidney transplant urgently so I gave her one of mine," the kind cowboy told us.

The girls were nearly crying from his tremendous generosity. With only one kidney left, it became too dangerous for the young man to continue throwing his body in front of 2000-pound bulls to save bull riders.

Saving his mother's life ultimately changed his life. "I don't regret it for a second. If I had to, I would do it again."

Recharged and full of delicious Brazilian treats, Kynan drove us back to the barn where the horses were resting and we hit the hay. The next day would be my last day in the saddle, and the last day had an early start! I put my head on the pillow, and Clara and I were so exhausted we passed out right away only to be awakened, what seemed like seconds later, by my phone's alarm.

"Today we finish this thing," I announced to Clara before she tried to keep me in bed a little longer.

It was still 3 a.m. and dark outside, but if we were to arrive at the Stampede Park on time for the special celebration they were putting on for us, we had to start immediately. I went to feed Mac and Smokey while Clara and Shelagh got breakfast ready. After they were fed, I brushed the boys. Dana Peers arrived with Mike Little and Ian Lister, who would be filming the day.

"Let's do this!" I said to Dana as we saddled our ponies.

"It's going to be a great day, Filipe!" Dana replied.

Finally, at 6:15 a.m., with the air still crisp and the sun coming up, I jumped into the saddle. With violet low-hanging stratus clouds over the Rockies to my right and a fire-lit sky to my left, I began the final twenty-seven kilometers of my journey across the Americas to Stampede Park in Calgary.

After trekking more than 25,000 kilometers through twelve nations over the past eight years, this was my last day in the saddle as a Long Rider. On that beautiful Friday, July 3, I wanted to look my best. I put on a freshly pressed white shirt and wore a present from the Stampede: a brand new 100x Smithbilt beaver pelt hat.

Astride Mac, with Clara beside me on Smokey, and the president of the Calgary Stampede, Dana Peers, riding a flashy palomino named Oz, we rode in silence. Clara looked stunning in a bright salmon button-up shirt, a brown leather jacket with fringes in the back (which used to belong to her mom Sandra), and a straight-brimmed, tan straw *gaucho* hat.

"What a dream," I said to her while we held hands atop our steeds. Her bracelet, the one I had given her in Patagonia three years earlier, sat on her left wrist, sparkling in the morning light.

From the saddle, I could see my El Dorado far off in the distance. Downtown Calgary was lit orange and gold by the rising sun. I was nervous as hell, and my horse could sense it. Mac pranced as we trekked south. The stunning buckskin sensed how tense I was as my heart tried to beat its way out of my chest. Smokey decided to ignore me and carried Clara with grace. Those two love each other.

Following Highway 1A south, two shadows appeared on the horizon. When we got closer, I realized the tall silhouettes were mounted police officers atop dark, glossy, and very wide horses. I was quickly transported to all those times that strangers rode out to greet me, to accompany me, and keep me safe. Hearty ranchers, farmers, shopkeepers, civil servants, poor sharecroppers, cartel members, lawmakers, millionaires, and nilionaires, people from all across humankind ready to help me fulfill my dream. It kept running through my head that this would be the final time.

"Good morning!" one of the officers said, a tall man in his early forties. "We will be accompanying you today as you ride into downtown Calgary." He almost tipped his helmet.

I grinned my thanks.

Mac displayed his jealousy of the two wide and big, black police horses by trying to bite and kick them. Smokey, on the other hand, scooted his way in between the large animals and pretended like he had been a police horse his entire life. The little gray looked like a pony next to the mighty animals.

We made a right turn onto 12 Mile Coulee Road, and I nearly froze. On both sides of the road sat long lines of vehicles while about fifty volunteers, police officers, and media personnel awaited our arrival.

As I stepped down from the saddle, an excited volunteer told me, "CTV, CBC, and Global Television are going to do live hits from here!"

Other volunteers held signs with messages on them:

Welcome Home!

Our Parade Marshal made it!

Go Filipe Go! YAHOOOOOO!

It was a stark contrast to the past few weeks on the road. Due to the COVID-19 pandemic, we had avoided civilization and followed the gravel Forestry Trunk Road from Hinton to Cochrane. In the middle of the Rockies and its foothills, we were surrounded by the wild. It was hard to imagine that only eight days ago, I was followed by a male grizzly near Corkscrew Mountain, and now I was being ambushed by the media here. Weirdly enough, I think I was less nervous with the bear.

After speaking to the media and thanking the Calgary Stampede volunteers who, even during this pandemic, continued to selflessly show the strength of their community spirit, we began crossing the cosmopolitan city.

"Make sure you take in every second." Dana smiled as we rode through sleepy subdivisions.

By 9:00 a.m., even though we weren't allowed to release our route in advance due to the pandemic, the streets were lined with Calgarians of all ages. Some were dressed in western gear. Bright smiles were stamped on some faces while others, hidden by masks, were content to observe from a socially correct distance. "Welcome home, Filipe!" I heard over and over again as I tried to contain the tempest brewing inside me.

The sky was now bright blue and cloudless. The Bow River ran to our right beside tall buildings that seemed to reach high into the sky. Little white balls of fluff carrying seeds from the nearby cottonwood trees floated by, making it look as if it were snowing.

As we rode, I leaned down to pat Mac's neck to thank him, but it was at that moment that the tears started to flow. I cried so hard, I began to hiccup. I couldn't control it or stop it. It was like everything I had felt and experienced these past eight years came pouring out of my soul at that moment.

On these journeys, I had a thousand homes. As I rode through Calgary, memories of all of them came flooding back. I was overwhelmed with images of the kindhearted people who hosted me with meals both lavish and humble, of the stunning places I saw, and the majestic horses I'd ridden.

This final journey took me through the truly breathtaking landscape of eastern Alaska and Northern and Western Canada. I spent time with the Osoyoos Indian Band and learned how to train wild horses from Master Horseman Aaron Stelkia. I rode next to Yukon's Kluane Lake, soaked in British Columbia's Laird Hot Springs, and struggled through a terrible snowstorm in the Rockies in the middle of summer. The clank of horseshoes, the creak of my saddle, and the rustle of leaves will always be the soundtrack to my life. The smell of horse sweat, my cologne.

The wildlife on this journey had been nothing short of amazing. I saw beavers, wolves, caribou, foxes, deer, elk, and a giant moose cow nursing her calf. In fact, I explored some of the seemingly endless uses of moose. I ate moose lasagna in Teslin, Yukon, and I attended the Adaka Cultural Festival in Whitehorse and learned how to make a moose hide canoe.

Most memorable, though, will always be the bears. I crossed paths with more bears than I could count in the southern Yukon, but the worst was a big menacing Albertan grizzly. Things are bigger in Alberta, and I'm sure he *knew* I ate bear meat pasta back in Toad River, B.C.!

Just after noon, I spotted Stampede Park over Mac's ears. It was eight years ago that I departed the Greatest Outdoor Show on Earth as an unknown cowboy with an impossible dream. Before I rode out on that hot July 8 in 2012, many people called me crazy. They said I wouldn't make it, that I would die. Now, here I was, returning as the Grand Marshal after having crossed the entirety of the Americas on horseback.

I reached for Clara's hand, and I thanked her for her commitment to this dream. "Without you, I wouldn't be here, *amor*," I told her as she wiped tears from her beautiful face.

I turned to Dana and saw that he, too, had teared up. "Thank you for believing in me, sir," I said to him before we embraced. He grinned and nodded. We didn't need any words.

When I stepped down from the saddle, my high school friend Shelagh's smile transported me home. Marie Aitken, who lent us the support vehicle for this final journey, hugged me tightly as tears ran down her face. Then I hugged Dana's wife Laura. For a second, it felt like I was hugging my own mother.

They were wonderful surrogates for my childhood friends and family who were not able to be there due to travel restrictions. But I felt their presence the entire time. My mom, dad, sisters, friends. They were all there in spirit and thought, along with Mancha, Gato, and Aimé Tschiffely, my childhood heroes, my inspiration, these souls who had changed my life.

After a live interview with Global Calgary, we made our way to the stage in the infield for the ceremony. The stands, which should have been packed with thousands of tourists from all over the world, sat empty and silent. It was an eerie scene in the midst of so much happiness.

Dana said a few words, then I tried to speak through my heavy tears and finally, Mayor Naheed Nenshi generously "White Hatted" me: Calgary's version of giving someone the key to the city. It's an honor I now share with the Queen of England, the Dalai Lama, Bob Dylan, Bill Clinton, and many other well-known visitors to that lovely city.

Before the ceremony came to an end, they made the mistake of giving me a bottle of champagne to pop. Enthusiastically, I did so, spraying everyone before taking a long sip of the bubbly drink, just like the late, great Brazilian racing legend Ayrton Senna after a particularly satisfying Formula-1 victory.

And then, like champagne suddenly released from its bottle after years of patiently waiting, the gratitude welled up in my heart and almost lifted me off the platform. Over the past eight years, hundreds, if not thousands, of people helped me fulfill this dream. Without them, I would never have left the spot where I now stood, much less return to it after the unforgettable adventure that will forever define my life.

Finally, I thanked Dana Peers, the Calgary Stampede and its selfless volunteers, the mounted police and motorcycle unit, the cops in patrol cars, the first responders, and the city of Calgary. Without them I wouldn't have been able to safely reach the finish line.

After the ceremony, it was time for more interviews and then to say a sad goodbye to our kids, Smokey and Mac. I'm so proud of these two majestic wild horses that I saw evolve from skittish equines into trusting animals. Their strength, resiliency, and horsepower allowed me to ride the final 800 kilometers from Grande Prairie to Calgary in only a month and ten days, a remarkable feat. They are the true heroes of this journey.

"I love you boys so much, and I'll see you soon. Now, you rest," I said before we loaded them up into the trailer. Clara and I would miss them greatly.

Since the news came out about Dana Peers choosing me as the 2020 Parade Marshal in early June, many people asked if I was heartbroken that the rodeo and parade were canceled, the first time in more than 100 years, the year I was to lead it all. The truth is, when I first heard about the cancellation in April, it did make me sad. But if there's one thing I have learned from my long rides, it's that positivity is one of the most important tools in life. It was the only reason I was able to take the first step back in 2012 and definitely why I arrived on time and alive in 2020.

When you believe in yourself, focus, plan, work hard, and stay positive, no matter what else is happening around you, your dreams can come true. If my Last Long Ride leaves you with only one thought, then let it be this: I hope you find the courage to follow your purpose and the strength to continue even if a global pandemic tries to rain on your parade. Always remember, in life, everyone carries a journey within them. Don't forget to start yours.

And when you finish that journey, start another!

26

THE FIRST DANCE

The day after our triumphant arrival in Calgary, I felt like a bus had run over me. "I don't think I can get out of bed," I told Clara before we shared a long kiss. The arrival was so emotional, I was completely and utterly drained. I cried so much my eyes were puffy and I felt dehydrated.

After a delicious breakfast at the fancy hotel the Calgary Stampede booked for us, Clara and I went to Dana and Laura's house.

"Welcome to your home for the next week," Laura announced over a delicious lunch she prepared for us.

After crossing more bears than I could count during the journey and never being attacked, I almost lost my finger to their tiny Pomeranian. Magnus was a small, light-brown and black miniature dog with the spunk of a grizzly. When I went to pet his fluffy little head after lunch, he nearly bit off my index finger and ate it as dessert.

"Are you bleeding?" Dana asked, laughing his head off. We all joined him.

That afternoon, Dana told me his friend Don Bell, one of the founders of WestJet, would fly us to see the Stampede Ranch in his helicopter. "You're going to love the ranch. There are more than 600 bucking horses living there," he said as his eyes lit up.

Sure, I was excited about seeing this legendary ranch and meeting those bucking machines, but when I heard the word helicopter, I only thought about one thing, "This is it!" This was the moment I had been waiting for. It was the perfect opportunity to ask the love of my life to spend the rest of our lives together. After meeting in Patagonia during my second Long Ride, dating for three years, and undertaking this Last Long Ride together, I would ask Clara to marry me at the Stampede Ranch. *My flor del Pago!*

When Clara was a little girl, her parents owned a helicopter business. They worked putting out forest fires, filming movies, and flew their chopper regularly. This sparked a strong passion in her for these flying machines. She could name the helicopters flying over us, sometimes just by the sound. "That's a Robinson R22," she would say.

Since the horse had literally brought us together when I rode into her arms in El Bolsón, a ranch with 600 of these majestic animals, some of the best bucking horses in the world, was the best place to pop the question. The thought alone made my heart jump into sixth gear.

With the help of Dana and Laura, I managed to shake off Clara and get to Spence Diamonds in Calgary the day prior to our flight.

"Hello, sir, how can I help you?" an East Indian man in a fancy black suit said to me when I walked into the sparkly store. He smelled expensive, like rose petals and champagne.

"Yes, sir, I need to buy a ring," I responded, realizing how stupid I sounded. Duh, everyone there was looking for a ring. That's what they sold.

"Great, we can definitely help you here. Do you know what style and price range you are looking for?"

After telling him I had no idea, he showed me some choices. As I looked around the ring selection, with about seventy models to choose from, I regretted my decision to come alone. I needed my mother.

"These will take about two weeks to be ready," he began to explain.

"Wait! Two weeks? No, I need it now. Like I have to buy the ring and walk out of here with it," I said to the now worried salesman.

"Oh, I see. Well, in that case you have to choose from one of these." He walked me over to a much smaller selection of twelve rings.

By the way he'd said, "Oh, I see," I felt like the employees called this pile "the crazy people rings." Thank God I never told him the story of how Clara and I met. He may have sent me to the insane asylum.

I called my mom and my friend Peter Hawkins on FaceTime and showed them my options. Luckily, we all agreed on one model. A delicate ring made of white gold with several diamonds on it. The top had two arches filled with small diamonds that went around the bigger rock on top, which made it look like a sideways 8, the infinity symbol.

"She's going to love it," Peter and my mother told me. After paying enough money to buy a Shining Spark filly, I walked out of the shop with a small black box holding the glittering ring.

Dana picked me up in his truck, and we went back to the house. From that point on, all I thought about was that black box and if I had hidden it well enough. I put it in a dirty sock deep in my luggage, the last place Clara would look. Or would she suddenly be inclined to wash our clothes, look for something she lost deep in our bag, or decide to organize our things? It was the most nerve-wracking twenty-four hours of my life.

The next morning, we woke early and went to Don's hangar to meet the legendary entrepreneur and pilot.

"Nice to meet you, Filipe and Clara," the tall, lean pilot said before we helped him push the chopper out of the hangar.

After a few minutes pushing buttons and pulling knobs and talking to flight control, we were off. Wearing my headset, I felt like I was Maverick in Top Gun, only I wasn't nervous about incoming

Russian MiGs. My mind was on the small black box, currently in Laura's purse. She was carrying the ring that would officially bind my life to my *flor del pago's*. I was a mess!

First, Don took us for a flight over the Stampede Grounds, which was epic, and then downtown Calgary. The one-hour flight to Hanna, Alberta, was absolutely beautiful as we flew over large ranches, the Badlands, and rolling hills.

When we landed at the 22,000-acre ranch, the family who lived there and took care of the animals greeted us warmly. "Welcome to the ranch, Filipe! We are happy to meet you and your wife," Tyler Kraft, one of the most talented pickup men and cowboys in the rodeo business, said to me. He might also have been a psychic. Wife? How did he know?

Over Tim Hortons coffee and donuts, we talked about the Born to Buck Program the Stampede started in the 1960s, the horses that live there, and daily life on the ranch. Next, Tyler took us to meet the legendary bucking horses, see the young guns coming up, and we visited the cemetery where the past legends were buried. The white tombstones showed the horses' names, the dates of birth and passing, and many flowers.

"These horses are true athletes. They're legends and to get to take care of them here on the ranch and travel to some of the biggest rodeos in North America with them is a dream come true," Tyler told me. His two little bleach-blond boys, both wearing oversized cowboy hats and boots, never left his side.

Before walking away from the cemetery, I asked Laura for the box and pocketed it in my Wrangler jeans pocket without Clara seeing. I whispered to my Italian mother that this was the time.

Under the ranch's main archway, a thick, bright red metal rectangle read: Calgary Stampede Ranch EST. 1961.

I handed my phone to Don and said, "Can you please take a photo of Clara and me in front of the ranch?"

I gave him a wink and he understood. Laura had given him a heads-up. I walked back to Clara and stood by her side as if we were posing for a photo.

I took a deep breath and started speaking, "I'm going to do something which I think is the most important moment of my life," I said in English before continuing in Spanish. At that moment, it dawned on me that I hadn't prepared anything to say, so I spoke from my heart.

"When I met you, you changed my life, *amor*, and I want to spend the rest of my life next to you. So..." I took one step back and began fishing for the box in my pocket. It was stuck. My Wrangler jeans didn't want to release the ring, but after a few seconds, I managed to pull it out.

Don said, "Oh my gosh!" from behind the camera while Clara covered her face with her hands.

I opened the box, dropped to my right knee, and looked up at the most gorgeous *gaucha* in the world. I spoke the four most important words of my life. "Clara, *quieres casar comigo?*" Clara, will you marry me?

"Síiiiiiiiiii!" she said before we hugged for what seemed like an eternity. We shared a long kiss.

With everyone cheering us, we looked deep into each other's eyes. At that moment, nothing else mattered but this *gaucha* in my arms and the excitement I felt for what the future would bring.

When I left Canada in 2012, I thought I was riding back to my home in Brazil. After 803 days in the saddle, I realized that I couldn't have been more wrong. When I arrived, I felt like a fish out of water. I went into a deep depression. I lost purpose. So, I'd set off again in search of something I didn't even know I was looking for: My *flor del pago*. My soulmate.

In the depths of the world, I met her in a windswept village. As soon as I looked into her powerful eyes, I fell in love. Together, we took on the far north and fell deeper in love. We became a team. During those past three years next to Clara, I realized that home is not a physical location on a map. It's a feeling you get deep in your heart. It's peace, tranquility, happiness, and love. It's all of this and more.

And it was all thanks to my wonderful horses who brought me

from Canada to Brazil, from Brazil to Patagonia — where my life changed forever — and finally home on our Last Long Ride.

I smiled at Clara. "They say home is where your heart is. Well, to me, home is wherever I'm with you."

ACKNOWLEDGMENTS

Can you imagine if I had never taken that first step into the unknown? If I hadn't put the naysayers and fear aside and stepped into that leather saddle on July 8 of 2012? Followed my instincts? Lived my purpose? My dream?

I wouldn't have written this trilogy, my story.

Luck doesn't exist! If that twenty-year-old kid hadn't had the courage to take that first step, to write it down and start the planning, I would not be the Filipe I am today. I would have cheated my destiny — my life's purpose!

What I learned from my Long Ride is that life is not easy for anybody. Everyone has problems. Limitations. Fears. But when you focus on saddling your horse and riding thirty kilometers a day, you can cross continents. It's not one big step, it's a million small hoof prints. And it starts with just one!

So, take the time to learn about who you are and what makes you happy. Have the courage to take the first step and the humility to ask for help.

And finally, believe in yourself! If you don't believe, no one else will! Now get on that horse and ride off into the unknown because life is too beautiful to stand still!

Thanks to:

Peter Hawkins, my mentor and friend who makes me better every day.

My mom Claudia, dad Iso, sisters Paolla and Izabella, my grandma Iolanda and my entire family who always supported me, no matter what.

My twelve majestic horses, Mac, Smokey, Bruiser, Dude, Frenchie, Life, Doll, Cautiva, Andariega, Sapito Gonzales, Texas, and Pablo Picasso, without whom this journey would never have been possible.

In memory of John Honderich. Thank you for everything, my man!

Special thanks:

Marie and Rocky Aitken, Dana and Laura Peers, The Calgary Stampede, Os Independentes, RG Rural, Viajar a Cavalo, Blueberry Farm, Arnon Melo, Naira Schiavon, MELLOHAWK Logistics, Jim McCrae, The Long Riders Guild, Aaron Stelkia and family, Osoyoos Indian Band, Sara Turner, Karen Hardy, Cole Barker, Tara O'Connel, Max O'Brien, Karen Hardy, Added Technology, Marcos Silva, Marcelo Murta, Saddle Up Clothing Company, Enlightened Equipment, CuChullaine O'Reilly, Pralana, Goyazes, Mike Little, Ian Lister, Jason Coxford, Steve McDonough, Will Osler, Stuart O'Connor, Mary Maw and family, Jocelyn Barrett, John and Sid Vandermeer, Lisa Dewhurst and family, Cindy Gillies, Kristina Barnes, Nevada Phipps, Robert Wise, Kenyan Vine, Saddle Up Clothing Company, and Penticton Indian Band.

And all of the wonderful families who hosted us from Alaska to Calgary! Thank you!

ABOUT THE AUTHOR

Filipe Masetti Leite is the youngest person and only fourth in the world to cross the Americas on horseback, an eight-year journey that took the Long Rider and his beloved horses across twelve nations, trekking more than 25,000 kilometres.

Two monuments have been erected in Brazil to celebrate his odyssey and his first pair of boots are on display at the Bata Shoe Museum in Toronto. In July of 2020, the journalist was chosen as the Calgary Stampede's Grand Marshal and White Hatted by Mayor Naheed Kurban Nenshi.

With more than 100k followers on social media, he writes for the *Toronto Star*, Canada's largest daily, worked with Rede Globo's *Fantastico* (Brazil's most watched Sunday night show), and in 2022, released a feature-length documentary on his epic Long Ride (Super Channel Canada).

The Long Rider has been selected by international film festivals around the world and garnered several awards. His best-sellers *Long Ride Home* (soon to be a major motion picture) and *Long Ride to the End of the World* are available in Portuguese and English on Amazon.

Follow Filipe on social media @filipemasetti and his award winning documentary *The Long Rider* @thelongriderfilm